PRESENTED TO:

_____

PRESENTED BY:

_____

DATE:

_____

Everything Christmas
Published by WaterBrook Press
12265 Oracle Boulevard, Suite 200
Colorado Springs, Colorado 80921

ISBN: 978-0-307-72929-3
ISBN: 978-0-307-72930-9 (electronic)

Copyright © 2010 by Bordon-Winters LLC
Project Compilation: Patricia Lutherbeck in association with SnapdragonGroup[SM] Editorial Services
The compiler has sought to locate and secure permission for the inclusion of all copyrighted material in this book. If any such acknowledgments have been inadvertently omitted, the compiler and publisher would appreciate receiving the information so that proper credit may be given in future editions.

Library of Congress Cataloging-in-Publication Data
Bordon, David.
    Everything Christmas / David Bordon, Tim Winters. —1st ed.
       p. cm.
    Includes index.
    ISBN 978-0-307-72929-3—ISBN 978-0-307-72930-9 (electronic) 1. Christmas. 2. Christmas—Miscellanea.
I. Winters, Tom. II. Title.
    GT4985.B59 2010
    394.2663—dc22

                                          2010027344

Printed in the United States of America
2010—First Edition

10 9 8 7 6 5 4 3 2 1

Special Sales
Most WaterBrook Multnomah books are available at special quantity discounts when purchased in bulk by corporations, organizations, and special-interest groups. Custom imprinting or excerpting can also be done to fit special needs. For information, please e-mail SpecialMarkets@WaterBrookMultnomah.com or call 1-800-603-7051.

Everything Christmas

WATERBROOK
PRESS

*Happy, happy Christmas, that can win us back
to the delusions of our childhood days, recall to the
old man the pleasures of his youth, and transport the
traveler back to his own fireside and quiet home!*

CHARLES DICKENS

*I wish we could put up some of the Christmas spirit in
jars and open a jar of it every month.*

HARLAN MILLER

It's All about Christmas

A well-known Christmas song called it "the most wonderful time of the year!" And there's not a better way to celebrate the joy of the season than with the very best of Christmas, past and present. This Christmas collection brings "everything Christmas" together in one volume for the entire family!

Everything Christmas offers you a potpourri of Christmas delights. Imagine being able to read favorite classic stories, learn the histories of our favorite Christmas traditions and new ways to celebrate them, and enjoy the words to treasured hymns and carols—complete with the stories behind them. You will be fascinated to discover how Christmas is celebrated at dinner tables around the world and to be introduced to new holiday recipes for your family get-togethers. You will find ideas for gift giving and seasonal crafts you can do alone or with little helpers—and even something to tickle your funny bone. All this is in addition to inspiring quotes, Scriptures, poems, and special Christmas remembrances.

The book is divided into daily chapters that you can use as an Advent calendar, on your own or with your family, to count down the days until Christmas. A topical index in the back will help you find favorite stories or recipes.

It's all about Christmas! Enjoy!

December 1

LET US KEEP CHRISTMAS
GRACE NOLL CROWELL

Whatever else be lost among the years,
Let us keep Christmas still a shining thing;
Whatever doubts assail us, or what fears,
Let us hold close one day, remembering
It's poignant meaning for the hearts of men.
Let us get back our childlike faith again.

The History of Christmas

Many of our Christmas traditions were celebrated centuries before the Christ child was born. The twelve days of Christmas, the bright fires, the yule log, gift giving, carnivals, carolers going from house to house, holiday feasts, even church processions can all be traced back to the early Mesopotamians. These traditions were passed down throughout the known world and were popular in Rome long before the birth of Christ.

Most historians say that some three centuries after the birth of Christ, Christianity was spreading rapidly. Church leaders were alarmed that their converts continued to honor the ancient celebrations honoring pagan gods. Early Christians had chosen to keep the birth of their Christ child a solemn and religious holiday, without merriment. For centuries they had forbidden their members to take part in those ancient celebrations. But now it seemed it was a losing battle. As a compromise, they agreed to allow their members to partake in a demure and respectful celebration of the birth of Christ. Thus, the Christian celebration we know as Christmas was born in Rome, near the date 336 AD.

The actual date of Christ's birth is unknown, so the early Christians chose December 25, probably to compete with the wildly popular Roman festival of Saturnalia. Eventually, most of the customs from the festival of Saturnalia were adopted into the celebration of Christmas and given new and sacred meanings.

Today, Christmas is both a holiday and a holy day. In America, it is the biggest event of the year, celebrated by people of all ages.

CHRISTMAS EVERY DAY

WILLIAM DEAN HOWELLS

*T*he little girl came into her papa's study, as she always did Saturday morning before breakfast, and asked for a story. He tried to beg off that morning, for he was very busy, but she would not let him. So he began:

"Well, once there was a little pig—"

She stopped him at the word. She said she had heard little pig stories till she was perfectly sick of them.

"Well, what kind of story *shall* I tell, then?"

"About Christmas. It's getting to be the season."

"Well!" Her papa roused himself. "Then I'll tell you about the little girl that wanted it Christmas every day in the year. How would you like that?"

"First-rate!" said the little girl; and she nestled into comfortable shape in his lap, ready for listening.

"Very well, then, this little pig—Oh, what are you pounding me for?"

"Because you said little pig instead of little girl."

"I should like to know what's the difference between a little pig and a little girl that wanted Christmas every day!"

"Papa!" said the little girl warningly. At this her papa began to tell the story.

Once there was a little girl who liked Christmas so much that she wanted it to be Christmas every day in the year, and as soon as Thanksgiving was over she began to send postcards to the old Christmas Fairy to ask if she mightn't have it. But the old Fairy never answered, and after a while the little girl found out that the Fairy wouldn't notice anything but real letters sealed outside with a monogram—or your initial, anyway. So, then, she began to send letters, and just the day before Christmas, she got a letter from the

Fairy, saying she might have it Christmas every day for a year, and then they would see about having it longer.

The little girl was excited already, preparing for the old-fashioned, once-a-year Christmas that was coming the next day. So she resolved to keep the Fairy's promise to herself and surprise everybody with it as it kept coming true, but then it slipped out of her mind altogether.

She had a splendid Christmas. She went to bed early, so as to let Santa Claus fill the stockings, and in the morning she was up the first of anybody and found hers all lumpy with packages of candy, and oranges and grapes, and rubber balls, and all kinds of small presents. Then she waited until the rest of the family was up, and she burst into the library to look at the large presents laid out on the library table—books, and boxes of stationery, and dolls, and little stoves, and dozens of handkerchiefs, and inkstands, and skates, and photograph frames, and boxes of watercolors, and dolls' houses—and the big Christmas tree, lighted and standing in the middle.

She had a splendid Christmas all day. She ate so much candy that she did not want any breakfast, and the whole forenoon the presents kept pouring in that had not been delivered the night before, and she went round giving the presents she had got for other people, and came home and ate turkey and cranberry for dinner, and plum pudding and nuts and raisins and oranges, and then went out and coasted, and came in with a stomachache crying, and her papa said he would see if his house was turned into that sort of fool's paradise another year, and they had a light supper, and pretty early everybody went to bed cross.

The little girl slept very heavily and very late, but she was wakened at last by the other children dancing around her bed with their stockings full of presents in their hands. "Christmas! Christmas! Christmas!" they all shouted.

"Nonsense! It was Christmas yesterday," said the little girl, rubbing her eyes sleepily.

Her brothers and sisters just laughed. "We don't know about that. It's Christmas today, anyway. You come into the library and see."

Then all at once it flashed on the little girl that the Fairy was keeping her promise, and her year of Christmases was beginning. She was dreadfully sleepy, but she sprang up and darted into the library. There it was again! Books, and boxes of stationery, and dolls, and so on.

There was the Christmas tree blazing away, and the family picking out their presents, and her father looking perfectly puzzled, and her mother ready to cry. "I'm sure I don't see how I'm to dispose of all these things," said her mother, and her father said it seemed to him they had had something just like it the day before, but he supposed he must have dreamed it. This struck the little girl as the best kind of a joke, and so she ate so much candy she didn't want any breakfast, and went round carrying presents, and had turkey and cranberry for dinner, and then went out and coasted, and came in with a stomachache, crying.

Now, the next day, it was the same thing over again, but everybody getting crosser, and at the end of a week's time so many people had lost their tempers that you could pick up lost tempers anywhere, they perfectly strewed the ground. Even when people tried to recover their tempers they usually got somebody else's, and it made the most dreadful mix.

The little girl began to get frightened, keeping the secret all to herself, she wanted to tell her mother, but she didn't dare to, and she was ashamed to ask the Fairy to take back her gift, it seemed ungrateful and ill-bred. So it went on and on, and it was Christmas on St. Valentine's Day and Washington's Birthday, just the same as any day, and it didn't skip even the First of April, though everything was counterfeit that day, and that was some little relief.

After a while turkeys got to be awfully scarce, selling for about a thousand dollars apiece. They got to passing off almost anything for turkeys—even half-grown hummingbirds. And cranberries—well they asked a diamond apiece for cranberries. All the woods and orchards were cut down for Christmas trees. After a while they had to make Christmas trees out of rags. But there were plenty of rags, because people got so poor, buying presents for one another, that they couldn't get any new clothes, and they just wore their old ones to tatters. They got so poor that everybody had to go to the poorhouse, except the confectioners, and the storekeepers, and the book sellers, and they all got so rich and proud that they would hardly wait upon a person when he came to buy. It was perfectly shameful!

After it had gone on about three or four months, the little girl, whenever she came into the room in the morning and saw those great ugly, lumpy stockings dangling at the fireplace, and the disgusting presents around everywhere, used to sit down and burst out crying. In six months she was perfectly exhausted, she couldn't even cry anymore.

And now it was on the Fourth of July! On the Fourth of July, the first boy in the United States woke up and found out that his firecrackers and toy pistol and two-dollar collection of fireworks were nothing but sugar and candy painted up to look like fireworks. Before ten o'clock every boy in the United States discovered that his July Fourth things had turned into Christmas things and was so mad. The Fourth of July orations all turned into Christmas carols, and when anybody tried to read the Declaration of Independence, instead of saying, "When in the course of human events it becomes necessary," he was sure to sing, "God rest you merry gentlemen." It was perfectly awful.

About the beginning of October the little girl took to sitting down on dolls wherever she found them—she hated the sight of them so, and by Thanksgiving she just slammed her presents across the room. By that time people didn't carry presents around nicely anymore. They flung them over the fence or through the window, and, instead of taking great pains to write "For dear Papa," or "Mama " or "Brother," or "Sister," they used to write, "Take it, you horrid old thing!" and then go and bang it against the front door.

Nearly everybody had built barns to hold their presents, but pretty soon the barns overflowed, and then they used to let them lie out in the rain, or anywhere. Sometimes the police used to come and tell them to shovel their presents off the sidewalk or they would arrest them.

Before Thanksgiving came it had leaked out who had caused all these Christmases. The little girl had suffered so much that she had talked about it in her sleep, and after that hardly anybody would play with her, because if it had not been for her greediness it wouldn't have happened. And now, when it came Thanksgiving, and she wanted them to go to church, and have turkey, and show their gratitude, they said that all the turkeys had been eaten for her old Christmas dinners and if she would stop the Christmases, they would see about the gratitude. And the very next day the little girl began sending letters to the Christmas Fairy, and then telegrams, to stop it. But it didn't do any good, and then she got to calling at the Fairy's house, but the girl that came to the door always said, "Not at home," or "Engaged," or something like that, and so it went on till it came to the old once-a-year Christmas Eve. The little girl fell asleep, and when she woke up in the morning—

"She found it was all nothing but a dream," suggested the little girl.

"No indeed!" said her papa. "It was all every bit true!"

"What *did* she find out, then?"

"Why, that it wasn't Christmas at last, and wasn't ever going to be, anymore. Now it's time for breakfast."

The little girl held her papa fast around the neck.

"You shan't go if you're going to leave it so!"

"How do you want it left?"

"Christmas once a year."

"All right," said her papa, and he went on again.

Well, with no Christmas ever again, there was the greatest rejoicing all over the country. People met together everywhere and kissed and cried for joy. Carts went around and gathered up all the candy and raisins and nuts, and dumped them into the river, and it made the fish perfectly sick. And the whole United States, as far out as Alaska, was one blaze of bonfires, where the children were burning up their presents of all kinds. They had the greatest time!

The little girl went to thank the old Fairy because she had stopped its being Christmas, and she said she hoped the Fairy would keep her promise and see that Christmas never, never came again. Then the Fairy frowned, and said that now the little girl was behaving just as greedily as ever, and she'd better look out. This made the little girl think it all over carefully again, and she said she would be willing to have it Christmas about once in a thousand years, and then she said a hundred, and then she said ten, and at last she got down to one. Then the Fairy said that was the good old way that had pleased people ever since Christmas began, and she was agreed. Then the little girl said, "What're your shoes made of?" And the Fairy said, "Leather." And the little girl said, "Bargain's done forever," and skipped off, and hippity-hopped the whole way home, she was so glad.

"How will that do?" asked the papa.

"First-rate!" said the little girl, but she hated to have the story stop, and was rather sober. However, her mama put her head in at the door and asked her papa:

"Are you never coming to breakfast? What have you been telling that child?"

"Oh, just a tale with a moral."

The little girl caught him around the neck again.

"*We* know! Don't you tell *what*, papa! Don't you tell *what*!" ✳

WILLIAM DEAN HOWELLS (1837–1920)

Best known as an editor and critic, this American fiction writer produced more than forty novels and story collections. He challenged American authors to choose American subjects, portray them honestly, and create characters who use native-American speech. As a critic, he helped to introduce writers like Mark Twain, Hamlin Garland, and Stephen Crane to American readers.

What is Christmas? It is tenderness for the past,
courage for the present, hope for the future.
It is a fervent wish that every cup may overflow
with blessings rich and eternal, and that
every path may lead to peace.

AGNES M. PHARO

SCENTED APPLESAUCE-CINNAMON ORNAMENTS

3 cups applesauce

3 cups ground cinnamon

Mix applesauce and cinnamon together until it is thick enough to hold a form. Flatten the mixture on a flat surface and cut into cookie-cutter shapes.

Place cookie shapes on a cookie sheet to dry for 3 to 4 days depending on the size and thickness of the cookies. If using as a hanging ornament, make a hole with a toothpick before drying. Makes 15 ornaments.

Chestnut Dressing

8 Tbsp. butter

3 ribs celery with leaves, chopped

16 ounces chestnuts

1 large chopped onion

$1/4$ cup chopped parsley

1 pound sourdough bread, cubed

3 cups turkey stock

Preheat oven to 400°F. Cut a deep X into the flattest side of each chestnut and place in a single layer on a baking sheet. Bake 30 minutes, or until outer skin of chestnut splits. Wrap roasted chestnuts in a towel to keep warm. Peel off the tough outer skin of the chestnut and thinner inner skin with a sharp knife. Chop the chestnuts coarsely and set aside.

Melt butter in a large skillet over medium heat. Add onion and celery and cook, stirring occasionally, for 10 minutes. Empty skillet contents into a large bowl. Add cubed bread, parsley, and enough stock to moisten the mix, about $2 1/2$ cups. Stir in chestnuts and add salt and pepper to taste.

Use to stuff poultry or place in a buttered baking dish, drizzle with $1/2$ cup more stock, and bake 30 minutes to an hour.

Makes 10–11 cups.

Roasted Goose

1 goose, 10–12 pounds

1 orange, halved

kosher salt and black pepper, to taste

For giblet stock (used in gravy):

2 onions, quartered

1 carrot, chopped

2 celery stalks, chopped

2 pints of water

2 sprigs of sage

2 sprigs fresh thyme

1 Tbsp. cornstarch (to thicken)

The goose should be defrosted and left at room temperature for at least 2 or 3 hours before cooking to bring it to equilibrium. This will improve the overall texture of the finished product. Remove the giblets from the goose and set aside. Wash the bird thoroughly inside and out with cool water and pat dry with a kitchen towel. Cut away any loose pieces of fat. Then rub the orange inside and outside of the bird. Mix the salt and pepper and rub into the skin and inside the cavity of the bird to season it.

Preheat the oven to 425°F.

Truss the bird by folding the wings back under the body.

Then tie the legs together with butcher's twine. Lightly prick the skin of the bird several times with a fork to allow the fat to adequately render during the cooking process. It is important not to pierce the flesh of the bird. Place the goose breast-side up on a rack in the roasting pan, and bake in the oven for approximately 30 minutes to develop some initial color. Then reduce the oven temperature to 325°F and continue cooking for approximately 3 hours.

Make a simple giblet stock to fortify and enrich the gravy while the goose is roasting by placing the giblets in a saucepan with some goose fat and cooking over low heat until browned. Add chopped onion, carrot, celery, herbs, and water. Bring to a boil and then simmer gently for about one hour. Strain and cool until needed.

The goose is done when the internal temperature of the thigh reaches 175°F. For a visual test to see if the goose is cooked, insert a skewer into the thickest part of the thigh. If the juices run clear, then it is ready. If not, then return to the oven for additional roasting time.

Once the goose is cooked, allow it to rest for 20–30 minutes. This will allow the meat to firm up and will help retain the juiciness of the bird. Remove all of the drippings from the roasting pan, strain, and remove the fat. Add these defatted drippings to the giblet broth and season to taste. To thicken the gravy, combine 1 Tbsp. of cornstarch with 3 Tbsp. of water and add to the gravy. Bring to a boil and simmer for 1–2 minutes or until thickened.

O Little Town of Bethlehem

Phillips Brooks

O little town of Bethlehem, how still we see thee lie!
Above thy deep and dreamless sleep the silent stars go by.
Yet in thy dark streets shineth the everlasting Light;
The hopes and fears of all the years are met in thee tonight.

For Christ is born of Mary, and gathered all above,
While mortals sleep, the angels keep their watch of wondering love.
O morning stars together, proclaim the holy birth,
And praises sing to God the King, and peace to men on earth!

How silently, how silently, the wondrous Gift is giv'n;
So God imparts to human hearts the blessings of His heav'n.
No ear may hear His coming, but in this world of sin,
Where meek souls will receive Him still, the dear Christ enters in.

Where children pure and happy pray to the blessed Child,
Where misery cries out to Thee, Son of the mother mild;
Where charity stands watching and faith holds wide the door,
The dark night wakes, the glory breaks, and Christmas comes once more.

O holy Child of Bethlehem, descend to us, we pray;
Cast out our sin, and enter in, be born in us today.
We hear the Christmas angels the great glad tidings tell;
O come to us, abide with us, our Lord Emmanuel!

On Christmas Eve, 1865, Phillips Brooks was in Jerusalem, a trip intended to inspire spiritual rebirth after the horrors of the Civil War. Just a few months earlier, he had spoken at the funeral of President Abraham Lincoln. That clear night as he walked the streets of the Holy City, he had a sudden inspiration. Renting a horse, he set out for Bethlehem. After a solitary journey under the clear night sky, Brooks reached the tiny, remote village and was surrounded by the spirit of the first Christmas. His impoverished soul was refreshed as he considered what had happened there so many years before. Three years later on Christmas Eve, 1868, as he sat alone in his study preparing his sermon for the next day, he felt inspired to pen the words to this beautiful carol.

I, the LORD All-Powerful,
will send my messenger
to prepare the way for me.
Then suddenly the Lord
you are looking for
will appear in his temple.
The messenger you desire
is coming with my promise,
and he is on his way.
(Malachi 3:1, CEV)

December 2

THE MERRY FAMILY GATHERINGS

HELEN LOWRIE MARSHALL

The merry family gatherings
The old, the very young;
The strangely lovely way they
Harmonize in carols sung.
For Christmas is tradition time
Traditions that recall
The precious memories down the years,
The sameness of them all.

1932 ROYAL CHRISTMAS MESSAGE

KING GEORGE V AND RUDYARD KIPLING

The first of the Royal Christmas Messages, written by Rudyard Kipling and broadcast live over radio from Sandringham House by King George V in 1932.

Through one of the marvels of modern science, I am enabled, this Christmas Day, to speak to all my peoples throughout the Empire. I take it as a good omen that wireless should have reached its present perfection at a time when the Empire has been linked in closer union. For it offers us immense possibilities to make that union closer still.

It may be that our future may lay upon us more than one stern test. Our past will have taught us how to meet it unshaken. For the present, the work to which we are all equally bound is to arrive at a reasoned tranquility within our borders; to regain prosperity without self-seeking; and to carry with us those whom the burden of past years has disheartened or overborne.

My life's aim has been to serve as I might, toward those ends. Your loyalty, your confidence in me has been my abundant reward.

I speak now from my home and from my heart to you all. To men and women so cut off by the snows, the desert, or the sea, that only voices out of the air can reach them; to those cut off from fuller life by blindness, sickness, or infirmity; and to those who are celebrating this day with their children and grandchildren.

To all—to each—I wish a Happy Christmas. God Bless You! ✴

CHRISTMAS DINNER IN ENGLAND

Traditional English Menu
Roast turkey
Stuffing and gravy
Roast potatoes
Vegetables
Bread sauce
Cranberry sauce
Christmas pudding with brandy sauce

The History
- In medieval England, peacocks and swans were eaten only by the rich at Christmas, but boar's head was the main course. In the eighteenth century, turkey, along with beef, slowly replaced the boar's head as most people's Christmas meal.
- The Christmas pudding was a porridge called "frumenty," a dish made of wheat or corn boiled in milk. As time went on, other ingredients, such as dried plums or prunes, eggs, and lumps of meat, were added to make it more interesting. When cooked, it was poured into a dish. This pudding was called "plum pudding."
- Update: Today, a Christmas pudding is a brown pudding with raisins, nuts, and dried fruit. It is served with custard or brandy butter. Often brandy is poured over the pudding, which is then set alight as it is carried to the table. The lights are turned off so people can see the dramatic dessert.

Did You Know?
- The turkeys on the English Christmas dining table were, for the most

part, imported from France by the Jesuits. In some French dialects, the turkey is still called a "Jesuite." Imagine hearing, "Pass the Jesuite, please!"

- It was the custom to hide silver coins in the Christmas pudding, promising good fortune for those who found them.
- In the beginning, Christmas pudding looked more like soup with raisins floating around in it.
- A Christmas cracker (firecracker) is placed next to each plate on the Christmas dinner table. When the crackers are pulled, out falls a colorful party crown, a toy or gift, and a festive joke.
- In medieval England, some celebrants followed the tradition of baking a giant, 165-pound pie. The giant pie was nine feet in diameter. Its ingredients included 2 bushels of flour, 20 pounds of butter, 4 geese, 2 rabbits, 4 wild ducks, 2 woodcocks, 6 snipes, 4 partridges, 2 neats' tongues, 2 curlews, 6 pigeons, and 7 blackbirds.

For Our English Friends: Have a *slap-up* meal—which means to eat well. The expression originates from the time of Charles Dickens, when it was a "slap-bang" meal, derived from cheap eating houses, where one's money was *slapped down* as the food was *banged* on the table. Probably to emphasize the difference in food quality in higher-class establishments, "down" became "up."

Did You Know?
"Rudolph, the Red-Nosed Reindeer" was conceived by author Robert May in 1939. Two other names he considered before deciding on Rudolph were Reginald and Rollo.

Glazed Ham

1 boneless ham, 4–6 pounds
1/4 cup plus 2 Tbsp. maple syrup
1 Tbsp. cornstarch
2 Tbsp. prepared mustard
1 cup water
1/2 tsp. pepper

Preheat the oven to 325°F. Place the ham in a roasting pan and cook for 45 minutes to warm the meat. Next, mix the maple syrup, cornstarch, mustard, water, and pepper together to make a glaze. Brush half of the glaze over the ham and bake for an additional 15–20 minutes. Repeat with the rest of the glaze and continue to bake for at least another 15 minutes, until the glaze is bubbly and has formed an even coat over the ham. Baste as needed.

POTATO STUFFING

3 pounds potatoes, peeled and diced
1 small onion, chopped
3 eggs
2 cups milk
3 cups bread, cubed
1 Tbsp. fresh sage, chopped
$1/4$ cup butter, cut into pieces

Preheat oven to 350°F. Boil the potatoes to begin the cooking process, approximately 15 minutes. Combine the partially cooked potatoes with remaining ingredients and pour into a large casserole dish. Bake for 45 minutes, uncovered, until browned.

COLORFUL PINE CONES
FOR THE FIREPLACE

Choose one of the chemicals listed below (which can be purchased at your local hardware or home improvement store) :

Blue fame = barium nitrate or copper sulfate

Red flame = strontium nitrate

Orange flame = calcium chloride

Green flame = copper chloride

Purple flame = lithium chloride or potassium permanganate

Rubber gloves

Disposable pan

Pine cones

Cloth sack

Thick stack of newspapers

Wearing your rubber gloves, mix 1 pound of the chemical in 1 gallon of water. Use only one salt or compound for color at a time on one group of pine cones. Mixing could cause toxic fumes.

Place the cones in a cloth sack and immerse them in the solution for half an hour. Hold the sack over a thick stack of newspapers to drain off the excess. Spread the pine cones out on newspaper to dry. Be sure to read and adhere to any warning labels on the chemicals, and never allow children to try this project without close supervision.

Add one or more to your fireplace for colorful flames!

THE WOODEN SHOES OF LITTLE WOLFF

FRANÇOIS COPPÉE

*O*nce upon a time—so long ago that the world has forgotten the date—in a city of the North of Europe—the name of which is so hard to pronounce that no one remembers it—there was a little boy, just seven years old, whose name was Wolff. He was an orphan and lived with his aunt, a hard-hearted, avaricious old woman, who never kissed him but once a year, on New Year's Day; and who sighed with regret every time she gave him a bowlful of soup.

The poor little boy was so sweet-tempered that he loved the old woman in spite of her bad treatment, but he could not look without trembling at the wart, decorated with four gray hairs, which grew on the end of her nose.

As Wolff's aunt was known to have a house of her own and a woolen stocking full of gold, she did not dare to send her nephew to the school for the poor. But she wrangled so that the schoolmaster of the rich boys' school was forced to lower his price and admit little Wolff among his pupils. The bad schoolmaster was vexed to have a boy so meanly clad and who paid so little, and he punished little Wolff severely without cause, ridiculed him, and even incited against him his comrades, who were the sons of rich citizens. They made the orphan their drudge and mocked at him so much that the little boy was as miserable as the stones in the street, and hid himself away in corners to cry—when the Christmas season came.

On the Eve of the great Day the schoolmaster was to take all his pupils to the midnight mass, and then to conduct them home again to their parents' houses.

Now as the winter was very severe, and a quantity of snow had fallen within the past few days, the boys came to the place of meeting warmly wrapped up, with fur-lined caps drawn down over their ears, padded jackets, gloves and knitted mittens, and good strong shoes with thick soles. Only little Wolff presented himself shivering in his thin everyday clothes, and wearing on his feet socks and wooden shoes.

His naughty comrades tried to annoy him in every possible way, but the orphan was so busy warming his hands by blowing on them, and was suffering so much from chilblains, that he paid no heed to the taunts of the others. Then the band of boys, marching two by two, started for the parish church.

It was comfortable inside the church, which was brilliant with lighted tapers. And the pupils, made lively by the gentle warmth, the sound of the organ, and the singing of the choir, began to chatter in low tones. They boasted of the midnight treats awaiting them at home. The son of the Mayor had seen, before leaving the house, a monstrous goose larded with truffles so that it looked like a black-spotted leopard. Another boy told of the fir tree waiting for him, on the branches of which hung oranges, sugar-plums, and punchinellos. Then they talked about what the Christ Child would bring them, or what he would leave in their shoes which they would certainly be careful to place before the fire when they went to bed. And the eyes of the little rogues, lively as a crowd of mice, sparkled with delight as they thought of the many gifts they would find on waking—the pink bags of burnt almonds, the bonbons, lead soldiers standing in rows, menageries, and magnificent jumping-jacks, dressed in purple and gold.

Little Wolff, alas! knew well that his miserly old aunt would send him to bed without any supper; but as he had been good and industrious all the year, he trusted that the Christ Child would not forget him, so he meant that night to set his wooden shoes on the hearth.

The midnight mass was ended. The worshipers hurried away, anxious to enjoy the treats awaiting them in their homes. The band of pupils, two by two, following the schoolmaster, passed out of the church.

Now, under the porch, seated on a stone bench, in the shadow of an arched niche, was a child asleep—a little child dressed in a white garment and with bare feet exposed to the cold. He was not a beggar, for his dress was clean and new, and—beside him upon the ground, tied in a cloth, were the tools of a carpenter's apprentice.

Under the light of the stars, his face, with its closed eyes, shone with an expression of divine sweetness, and his soft, curling blond hair seemed to form an aureole of light about his forehead. But his tender feet, blue with the cold on this cruel night of December, were pitiful to see!

The pupils so warmly clad and shod, passed with indifference before the unknown child. Some, the sons of the greatest men in the city, cast looks of scorn on the barefooted one. But little Wolff, coming last out of the church, stopped deeply moved before the beautiful, sleeping child.

"Alas!" said the orphan to himself, "how dreadful! This poor little one goes without stockings in weather so cold! And, what is worse, he has no shoe to leave beside him while he sleeps, so that the Christ Child may place something in it to comfort him in all his misery."

And carried away by his tender heart, little Wolff drew off the wooden shoe from his right foot, placed it before the sleeping child; and as best as he was able, now hopping, now limping, and wetting his sock in the snow, he returned to his aunt.

"You good-for-nothing!" cried the old woman, full of rage as she saw that one of his shoes was gone. "What have you done with your shoe, little beggar?"

Little Wolff did not know how to lie, and, though shivering with terror as he saw the gray hairs on the end of her nose stand upright, he tried, stammering, to tell his adventure.

But the old miser burst into frightful laughter. "Ah! the sweet young master takes off his shoe for a beggar! Ah! master spoils a pair of shoes for a barefoot! This is something new, indeed! Ah! well, since things are so, I will place the shoe that is left in the fireplace, and tonight the Christ Child will put in a rod to whip you when you wake. And tomorrow you shall have nothing to eat but water and dry bread, and we shall see if the next time you will give away your shoe to the first vagabond that comes along."

And saying this the wicked woman gave him a box on each ear, and made him climb to his wretched room in the loft. There the heartbroken little one lay down in the darkness, and, drenching his pillow with tears, fell asleep.

But in the morning, when the old woman, awakened by the cold and shaken by her cough, descended to the kitchen, oh! wonder of wonders! she saw the great fireplace filled with bright toys, magnificent boxes of sugar-plums, riches of all sorts, and in front of all this treasure, the wooden shoe which her nephew had given to the vagabond, standing beside the other shoe which she herself had placed there the night before, intending to put in it a handful of switches.

And as little Wolff, who had come running at the cries of his aunt, stood in speechless delight before all the splendid Christmas gifts, there came great shouts of laughter from the street.

The old woman and the little boy went out to learn what it was all about, and saw the gossips gathered around the public fountain. What could have happened? Oh, a most amusing and extraordinary thing! The children of all the rich men of the city, whose parents wished to surprise them with the most beautiful gifts, had found nothing but switches in their shoes!

Then the old woman and little Wolff remembered with alarm all the riches that were in their own fireplace, but just then they saw the pastor of the parish church arriving with his face full of perplexity.

Above the bench near the church door, in the very spot where the night before a child, dressed in white, with bare feet exposed to the great cold, had rested his sleeping head, the pastor had seen a golden circle wrought into the old stones. Then all the people knew that the beautiful, sleeping child, beside whom had lain the carpenter's tools, was the Christ Child himself, and that he had rewarded the faith and charity of little Wolff.✷

FRANÇOIS COPPÉE (1842–1908)
A renowned poet and dramatist, the author of this tale was most famous for his one-act play in which Sarah Bernhardt made her first appearance. Much of his work has a sentimental tone, especially those where he emphasized the sorrows of the poor. He also wrote several religious novels.

HAMLET: ACT 1, SCENE 1

WILLIAM SHAKESPEARE

Some say that ever 'gainst that season comes,
Wherein our Saviour's birth is celebrated,
The bird of dawning singeth all night long;
And then, they say, no spirit dares stir abroad;
The nights are wholesome;
then no planets strike
No fairy takes,
nor witch hath power to charm,
So hallowed, and so gracious is the time.

December 3

The coming of Christ by way of a
Bethlehem manger seems strange and stunning.
But when we take him out of the manger and invite
him into our hearts, then the meaning unfolds
and the strangeness vanishes.

Neil C. Strait

Princess Victoria's Diary

Christmas Eve, 1932

*A*fter dinner we went upstairs. I then saw Flora, the dog which Sir John was going to give Mamma. Aunt Sophia came also. We then went into the drawing room near the dining room. After Mamma had rung a bell three times we went in. There were two large round tables on which were placed two trees hung with lights and sugar ornaments. All the presents being placed round the tree.

I had one table for myself and the Conroy family had the other together. Lehzen had likewise a little table. Mamma gave me a little lovely pink bag which she had worked with a little sachet likewise done by her; a beautiful little opal brooch and earrings, books, some lovely prints, a pink satin dress and a cloak lined with fur. Aunt Sophia gave me a dress which she worked herself, and Aunt Mary a pair of amethyst earrings. Lehzen a lovely music-book. Victoire a pretty white bag worked by herself, and Sir John a silver brush.

Mamma then took me up into my bedroom with all the ladies. There was a new toilet table with a white muslin cover over pink and all my silver things standing on it with a fine new looking-glass. I stayed up till half past 9. ✳

CHRISTMAS DINNER IN POLAND

Traditional Polish Menu

Mushroom soup

Borscht (a vegetable stew)

Sledzie (pickled herring)

Fried fish (usually carp)

Pierogi (filled dumplings)

Cabbage rolls

Boiled potatoes

Beans and sauerkraut

Dried fruit compote

Kutia (pudding)

The History

- Dinner is served on Christmas Eve in Poland, not on Christmas Day.
- In honor of the Star of Bethlehem, the meal cannot begin until the first star of night appears.
- Bits of hay are spread beneath the tablecloth as a reminder that Christ was born in a manger.
- The meal begins with the breaking of the oplatek, a thin, rectangular, unleavened wafer. Everyone at the table breaks off a piece and eats it as a symbol of their unity with Christ.
- Twelve courses are served, one for each apostle and also for each month in the year.
- Kutia, a sweet grain pudding, is often the first dish in the traditional twelve-dish Christmas Eve supper.
- An empty place setting is left at the table for the baby Jesus or a wanderer who may come in need.

Did You Know?

- Though Christmas in Poland is officially known as Boze Narodzenie, it is most often referred to as Gwiazdka, which means, "Little star."
- According to tradition, no cooking is done on Christmas Day.
- Christmas dinner in Poland is known as Wigilia and is traditionally meatless.
- The Wigilia derives its name from the Latin word vigilare, which means "to watch or keep vigil."
- Every effort is made to ensure that there is an even number of people at the table on this sacred night. An odd number is thought to bring bad luck.

For Our Polish Friends: Remember to fill your heart with good-will and fast until the first star, Gwiazdka, appears in the sky. Tradition says that the family fasts as they toil in preparation for Christmas Day. Someone—usually the youngest child in the family—watches at the window for the appearance of the first star. When the star is spotted, the candles are lit in every window, and the Christmas celebration begins.

Thanks be to God for his unspeakable Gift—
Indescribable
Inestimable
Incomparable
Inexpressible
Precious beyond words.

LOIS LEBAR

ORANGE CRANBERRY SAUCE

2 pounds cranberries
2 Tbsp. orange zest
3 cinnamon sticks
1 pint orange juice
2 cups packed brown sugar
2 cups water

Place the cranberries, grated orange rind, cinnamon, orange juice, brown sugar, and enough water to cover cranberries in a saucepan. Bring mixture to a boil over high heat. Immediately turn heat down and simmer for about one hour or until the sauce has thickened. Taste for sweetness and adjust with additional sugar if necessary. You cannot overcook, so continue cooking until you have a good, thick consistency. Let mixture cool a bit, and then refrigerate in a covered container.

CHRISTMAS CARDS

History: Though wood engravers produced prints with religious themes in the European Middle Ages, the first commercial Christmas and New Year's card was designed in London, England, in 1843. The picture on the front—a family with a small child drinking wine together—turned out to be controversial, but the idea stuck.

John Callcott Horsley (1817-1903), a British narrative painter and a Royal Academician, designed the first Christmas and New Year's card at the suggestion and request of his friend Sir Henry Cole, who was the first director of the Victoria and Albert Museum. Horsley designed the first Christmas card in 1840, but it did not go on sale until 1843, when one thousand cards were offered for one shilling each. The Christmas card became very popular, and other artists quickly followed Horsley's concept.

Early English cards rarely showed winter or religious themes, favoring flowers, fairies, and other fanciful designs in honor of the approach of spring. Humorous and sentimental images of children and animals were popular, as well as increasingly elaborate shapes, decorations, and materials.

Louis Prang was the first printer to offer Christmas cards in America in 1875. The style and extravagance of the cards evolved throughout the twentieth century with changing printing techniques. Patriotic themes were popular during the world wars, and religious themes dominated starting with the 1950s.

Even though new technologies have caused a serious drop in the number of cards received by households, approximately 1.8 billion cards are sent annually.

Christmas Idea: In recent years, some families have opted to include a Christmas letter updating friends on the events of the past year. You might choose one person or merge the contributions of all the family members. This is especially easy when done on the computer.

Note: It's best to produce a letter with genuine news—letters that sound like press releases touting family achievements can be tiresome.

Christmas Idea: Some families have chosen to send a Christmas postcard containing a family photograph and printed greeting. This has become a very popular way of updating friends and family members who live far away with how the family is growing and maturing.

Christmas Idea: You might want to consider sending your Christmas letter in January, a current trend. After the hustle and bustle of celebrating is over, there is much more time to thoughtfully create a mail-out of better quality and meaning. Also, there is more time for the recipient to read it at their leisure.

Christmas Idea: Create a Christmas card tree by using a hole-puncher to put a hole in the top left corner of the card through both front and back. Tie the card to the tree with a ribbon. You might also want to place a Christmas basket on the coffee table or kitchen counter in which to place cards as they arrive, giving family members a chance to look at them. Handmade, particularly beautiful, and sentimental Christmas cards can be easily maintained in an album with favorite cards from past years.

Cornish Hens

8 Cornish hens, thawed
4 cups dry red wine
1 cup olive oil
4 cloves garlic, crushed
1/3 cup fresh sage, chopped
8 bacon slices, chopped
1/3 cup fresh chives, chopped
1 cup dry breadcrumbs
1/2 cup pine nuts
Kitchen string

Place Cornish hens in a bowl. Combine next 4 ingredients in another bowl. Pour over hens. Cover and marinate in refrigerator at least 3 hours, turning occasionally.

Combine next 4 ingredients in a bowl and mix thoroughly. Remove hens from marinade, reserving 2 cups of marinade. Preheat oven to 350°F. Spoon stuffing into hen cavities and secure legs with string. Place hens on a wire rack in a large roasting pan. Bake 1 hour, or until tender.

Meanwhile, bring reserved marinade to a boil in a pan. Simmer 4–5 minutes or until reduced by one third. Serve sauce with hens.

DECK THE HALLS!

AN OLD WELSH TUNE

Deck the halls with boughs of holly,
Fa la la la la, la la la la.
'Tis the season to be jolly,
Fa la la la la, la la la la.
Don we now our gay apparel,
Fa la la, la la la, la la la.
Troll the ancient Yuletide carol,
Fa la la la la, la la la la.

See the blazing Yule before us,
Fa la la la la, la la la la.
Strike the harp and join the chorus.
Fa la la la la, la la la la.
Follow me in merry measure,
Fa la la, la la la, la la la.
While I tell of Yuletide treasure,
Fa la la la la, la la la la.

Fast away the old year passes,
Fa la la la la, la la la la.
Hail the new, ye lads and lasses,
Fa la la la la, la la la la.
Sing we joyous, all together,
Fa la la, la la la, la la la.
Heedless of the wind and weather,
Fa la la la la, la la la la.

HISTORICAL NOTE:

The melody for this carol is derived from an old Welsh tune, which gained popularity in the 1700s. Mozart enjoyed playing it as a piano-violin duet. Sometime after 1800, the words were added as the tune became known in America. It is the classical model of the jolly, secular carol.

Christmas—that magic blanket that wraps itself about us, that something so intangible that it is like a fragance. It may weave a spell of nostalgia. Christmas may be a day of feasting, or of prayer, but always it will be a day of remembrance—a day in which we think of everything we have ever loved.

AUGUSTA E. RUNDEL

Born in a stable,
Cradled in a manger,
In the world His hands had made,
Born a stranger.

CHRISTINA ROSSETTI

December 4

*It is Christmas every time you let God love others
through you...yes, it is Christmas every time you smile
at your brother and offer him your hand.*

MOTHER TERESA OF CALCUTTA

Unlikely Places

Cheri Fuller

In 1975 our four-year-old son Justin was in a hospital in Tulsa, Oklahoma, recovering from a severe asthma attack. We had planned to spend a very traditional family Christmas at home, but as it turned out our young son was one of the few patients in the children's ward who was just too ill to be released. Despite our carefully laid plans, it had become evident that Justin, along with a few other sick youngsters and their parents, would not be going home for the holidays.

The whole hospital experience had been painful for Justin. I felt sorry for him. Instead of sitting on Santa's knee sharing his Christmas wish or hanging his stocking on the mantelpiece at home, there he was—stuck in a drab hospital, hooked up to an IV and caged by an oxygen tent.

Moreover, I was disappointed that my own last-minute plans for package-wrapping, cookie-baking, and stocking-stuffing had been spoiled. Being newcomers in town, we had no friends to visit us in the hospital, and despite the good intentions of the caring medical staff, a hospital was still a very lonely place to be at Christmas time.

I missed our other son, eighteen-month-old Christopher, who was at home with Dad in our family room which, when we left, had been all aglow with twinkling Christmas tree lights, gaily colored felt stockings all hung in a row, bright plaid bows, and shining candles. In contrast, Justin and I gazed for hours at the monotonous brown walls and faded curtains that blended so well with the gray hospital floors.

I felt angry and frustrated, but I didn't want to show it. I needed to help keep Justin's spirits up until we could get him back home. The family had decided to postpone Christmas until the day Justin returned. Until then, we would act as if Christmas hadn't yet arrived.

While we had expected to put Christmas off, God had other plans! Much to our surprise, He was to use this experience to teach us the true meaning of Christmas.

On Christmas Eve, God's love came first in the form of a man brightly dressed as Santa Claus. Bounding down the hall, he delivered a thoughtful, personal gift to each youngster. Justin was given a cowboy hat that, surprisingly, was just his size.

"Who is this from?" I asked the nurse in attendance. "Did some organization send this gift?"

I thought that perhaps some local civic club had done this as its yearly project.

"Oh, no," she replied. "Three years ago a mom and dad's only daughter, a little three-year-old, died in this ward on Christmas Eve. Now each year the parents bring special gifts to the children who have to stay in the hospital at Christmas. Although they prefer to remain anonymous, they still manage to obtain the exact size or need of each child."

While I was pondering this act of kindness, two little Campfire girls brought in a handmade white mitten ornament decorated with holly and presented it to Justin.

"Merry Christmas!" they chimed to us as they continued happily down the hall.

Hardly had the cheerful words faded away when a family of Mexican-American carolers arrived. Gaily dressed in red and green native costumes, guitars in hand, they sang to us of the "Silent Night."

Next a big University of Oklahoma football player in his red and white varsity jersey walked in and began to chat with Justin. An avid football fan, Justin couldn't believe that a "real live" gridiron hero had come especially to see him. He was all the more amazed and delighted when the burly athlete produced a surprise gift for him. Opening it, Justin beamed.

"A cowboy rifle and spurs!" he exclaimed excitedly. "They go with the hat!"

The coincidence took my breath away.

The next day, on Christmas morning, a tall, thin, shabbily dressed man quietly entered the room and sat on the edge of Justin's bed. Like some character from a Dickens novel, his clothes were tattered and torn. Without a word, he took out an old flute and began to play a lovely Christmas medley. One carol blended into another as the simplicity of each song took on a beauty beyond any I had ever known. Finishing his serenade like the little drummer boy, he handed Justin a small cup full of tiny red candles. Then with a smile he slipped out the door. He had said very little and had never identified himself.

Slowly, but clearly, I began to realize that none of the people who had shared their love and gifts with us knew us—or had even told us their names. We had done nothing to earn or deserve their gifts. While my own hurts and needs had created a cold barrier around my emotions, these simple acts of kindness had caused the walls of neglected feelings to come tumbling down.

That lonely hospital, with its drab walls lined with construction paper bells, had become a place of God's healing and reconciling love. Away from family, friends, and our baby son, without our family tree and familiar traditions, God had delivered to us His special Christmas gift. The loneliest and darkest of places had been filled with the presence of angels and the brightest of lights.[1] ✳

Holiday Peanut Brittle

2 cups sugar
2 cups raw peanuts
2 tsp. baking soda
1 cup white corn syrup
1 Tbsp. butter
1 tsp. vanilla

Bring 1/2 cup water to a boil. Add sugar and syrup. Boil until it spins a thread (300°F). Add peanuts and cook until golden brown. Remove from heat. Stir in soda, butter, and vanilla. Quickly spread onto 2 greased cookie sheets. Chill for about one hour, and then break apart.

Santa Stats

To deliver all his gifts in one night, Santa would have to make 822.6 visits per second (at three thousand times the speed of sound). At that speed, Santa and his reindeer would instantaneously burst into flames in Earth's atmosphere just like meteors.

> You, Bethlehem...out of you will come for me one who will be ruler over Israel. He will stand and shepherd his flock in the strength of the LORD, in the majesty of the name of the LORD his God. And they will live securely, for then his greatness will reach to the ends of the earth. And he will be their peace.
>
> (Micah 5:2, 4–5)

Did You Know?

The picture of a potbellied, bearded, and bell-ringing Father Christmas was created by Thomas Nast, a North American cartoonist, in drawings he made for *Harper's Weekly* during a period of twenty years from 1863 onward. He based the pictures on Clement Moore's poem, gradually developing Moore's small, fat, elf-like creature into the Father Christmas now known to all.

Did You Know?

Before settling on the name of Tiny Tim for his character in *A Christmas Carol*, Charles Dickens considered three alternative names. They were Little Larry, Puny Pete, and Small Sam.

A Christmas Carol

J. R. Lowell

"What means this glory round our feet?"
The Magi mused, "more bright than morn?"
And voices chanted clear and sweet,
"Today the Prince of Peace is born!"

"What means that star?" the shepherd said,
"That brightens through the rocky glen?"
And angels answering overhead,
Sang, "Peace on earth, good will to men!"

'Tis twenty hundred years and more
Since those sweet oracles were dumb;
We wait for Him, like them of yore;
Alas, He seems so slow to come!

But it was said, in words of gold.
No time or sorrow e'er shall dim,
That little children might be bold
In perfect trust to come to Him.

All round about our feet shall shine
A light like that the wise men saw,
If we our loving wills incline
To that sweet Life which is the Law.

So shall we learn to understand
The simple faith of shepherds then,
And clasping kindly hand in hand,
Sing, "Peace on earth, good will to men!"

And they who do their souls no wrong,
But keep at eve the faith of morn,
Shall daily hear the angel-song,
"Today the Prince of Peace is born!"

Did You Know?
Electric tree lights were first used just three years after Thomas Edison had his first mass public demonstration of electric lights in 1879. Thomas Edison's assistant, Edward Johnson, came up with the idea of electric lights for Christmas trees in 1882. His lights were a huge hit. It took quite a few years before they were available to the general public.

Did You Know?
The first American Christmas carol was written in 1649 by a minister named John de Brébeuf and is called "Jesus Is Born."

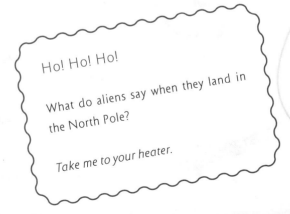

Ho! Ho! Ho!

What do aliens say when they land in the North Pole?

Take me to your heater.

"MERRY CHRISTMAS"
AROUND THE WORLD

African/Eritrean/Tigrinja: Rehus-Beal-Ledeats

Albanian: Gezur Krislinjden

Arabic: Milad Majid

Argentinian: Feliz Navidad

Armenian: Shenoraavor Nor Dari yev Pari Gaghand

Bengali: Shuvo Naba Barsha

Brazilian: Boas Festas e Feliz Ano Novo

Bulgarian: Tchestita Koleda; Tchestito Rojdestvo Hristovo

Chilean: Feliz Navidad

Chinese (Cantonese): Gun Tso Sun Tan'Gung Haw Sun

Chinese (Mandarin): Kung His Hsin Nien bing Chu Shen Tan

Choctaw: Yukpa, Nitak Hollo Chito

Croatian: Sretan Bozic

Czech: Prejeme Vam Vesele Vanoce a stastny Novy Rok

Danish: Glædelig Jul

Dutch: Vrolijk Kerstfeest en een Gelukkig Nieuwjaar! or Zalig
   Kerstfeast

English: Merry Christmas

Eskimo (inupik): Jutdlime pivdluarit ukiortame pivdluaritlo!

Estonian: Ruumsaid juuluplhi

Finnish: Hyvaa joulua

French: Joyeux Noël

German: Froehliche Weihnachten

Greek: Kala Christouyenna!

Hawaiian: Mele Kalikimaka

Hebrew: Mo'adim Lesimkha. Chena tova

Hungarian: Kellemes Karacsonyi unnepeket

Icelandic: Gledileg Jol

Indonesian: Selamat Hari Natal

Iraqi: Idah Saidan Wa Sanah Jadidah

Irish: Nollaig Shona Dhuit, or Nodlaig mhaith chugnat

Iroquois: Ojenyunyat Sungwiyadeson honungradon nagwutut. Ojenyunyat osrasay.

Italian: Buone Feste Natalizie

Japanese: Shinnen omedeto. Kurisumasu Omedeto

Korean: Sung Tan Chuk Ha

Latvian: Prieci'gus Ziemsve'tkus un Laimi'gu Jauno Gadu!

Navajo: Merry Keshmish

Norwegian: God Jul, or Gledelig Jul

Papiamento: Bon Pasco

Polish: Wesolych Swiat Bozego Narodzenia or Boze Narodzenie

Portuguese:Feliz Natal

Romanian: Sarbatori vesele

Russian: Pozdrevlyayu s prazdnikom Rozhdestva is Novim Godom

Slovakian: Sretan Bozic or Vesele vianoce

Serbian: Hristos se rodi

Spanish: Feliz Navidad

Swedish: God Jul and (Och) Ett Gott Nytt År

Thai: Sawadee Pee Mai

Turkish: Noeliniz Ve Yeni Yiliniz Kutlu Olsun

Ukrainian: Srozhdestvom Kristovym

Vietnamese: Chuc Mung Giang Sinh

Yugoslavian: Cestitamo Bozic

Roast Turkey

1 turkey, about 14 pounds
$1/4$ cup unsalted butter, melted
1 $1/3$ cups chicken stock

Preheat oven to 325°F. Season inside of turkey cavity with salt and pepper to taste. Pat skin dry with paper towels. Brush turkey with melted butter. Place turkey on a roasting rack inside a roasting pan. Roast turkey about 20 minutes per pound, basting with chicken stock and brushing with butter every 25 minutes, until a meat thermometer registers 175°F when inserted into thickest part of the thigh (or when thigh and leg fall easily away when pulled). Remove turkey from oven. Let turkey stand 20 minutes before carving.

Oyster Dressing

1 1/2 cups celery, chopped
2 large onions, chopped
1/4 pound butter
1 bag breadcrumbs, unseasoned
1/2 cup milk
2 eggs, beaten
Salt to taste
1 tsp. poultry seasoning
1/2 pint oysters, raw

Sauté celery and onion in butter until delicately browned. Add breadcrumbs and mix. To that mixture, add milk, eggs, and poultry seasoning and stir vigorously. Remove from heat before adding salt and oysters. Fold those into the other ingredients. Stuff into turkey and bake as you normally would.

Note: If you stuff the turkey the night before, be sure to refrigerate it until it is ready to go into the oven.

THE LITTLE LOAF

McGuffey's Third Reader

*O*nce, when there was a famine, a rich baker sent for twenty of the poorest children in the town and said to them, "In this basket there is a loaf for each of you. Take it, and come back to me every day till God sends us better times."

The hungry children gathered eagerly about the basket and quarreled for the bread, because each wished to have the largest loaf. At last they went away without even thanking the good man.

But Gretchen, a poorly dressed little girl, did not quarrel or struggle with the rest, but remained standing modestly a pace away. When the ill-behaved children had left, she took the smallest loaf, which alone was left in the basket, kissed the man's hand, and went home.

The next day the children were ill-behaved as before, and poor, timid Gretchen received a loaf scarcely half the size of the one she got the first day. When she came home, and her mother cut the loaf open, many new, shining pieces of silver fell out of it.

The mother was very much alarmed, and said, "Take the money back to the good man at once, for it must have got in the dough by accident. Go quickly, Gretchen, go quickly!"

But when the little girl gave the rich man her mother's message, he said, "No, no, my child, it was no mistake. I had the silver pieces put into the smallest loaf to reward you. Always be contented, peaceable, and grateful as you are now. Go home, now, and tell your mother that the money is your own."

Top Ten Favorite Christmas Toys of All Time for Boys

1. Video games
2. Matchbox cars
3. Legos
4. Electric trains
5. Swiss army knife
6. Toy soldiers
7. Bicycle
8. Skateboard
9. Construction set
10. Yo-yo

The kindness of Christmas is the kindness of Christ.
To know that God so loved us as to give us His Son for
our dearest Brother has brought human affection to its
highest tide on the day of that Brother's birth.
If God so loved us, how can we help loving one another?

MALTBIE DAVENPORT BABCOCK

December 5

*Unless we make Christmas an occasion
to share our blessings, all the snow in Alaska
won't make it "white."*

BING CROSBY

A REFUGEE CAMP CHRISTMAS

RENIE BURGHARDT

*D*uring World War II, we had many sad Christmases. Fear was always lurking in some near-by corner. Those were the times we mainly observed Christmas in our hearts. So when in 1947 we arrived in the refugee camp in Austria, just a few weeks before Christmas, I wasn't expecting anything different. At age eleven, I had become resigned to not having much.

The refugee camp, with its wooden barracks, and dusty lanes, was pretty drab. But we had a warm place to sleep, warm food to eat, and were outfitted with warm clothes donated toward the refugee effort from various generous-minded countries like the United States, Canada, and Great Britain. We considered ourselves pretty fortunate. And we had some of the most beautiful views available, free to anyone who wished to look, since the camp was located in one of the most scenic areas of Austria—Carinthia.

As Christmas was approaching, the refugee camp school I attended made plans to help us celebrate the holiday as a group. In the barracks we lived in, our private spaces were tiny cubicles, where we slept. There was no room for individual celebrations. But the school had a large auditorium, where a donated Christmas tree was set up, which we, the children, helped decorate with our own hand-made ornaments. There were candles on the tree too, which were to be lit Christmas Eve, just like it used to be done in Hungary, before the war. And we were rehearsing the school Christmas play, to be presented on Christmas Eve. I had a small part in the play—the angel who comes to give the message to the shepherds about the birth of the Savior. I was very pleased and excited about the part.

On Christmas Eve afternoon, my grandparents and I decided to take a walk to the small town of Spittal, just a few miles from the camp. Grandfather felt that even though we had no money to buy anything, taking in the Christmas sights and smells would be worth the walk. The town's cobbled streets, with its many small shops, were decorated with fir branches, and small trees in shop windows glowed with lit candles. People were hustling and bustling, getting last minute things for the holiday, and wishing each other "Froliche Weinachten." We stopped in front of the bakery and inhaled the delicious smells coming out of it every time someone opened the door. I gazed at the Napoleons, displayed in the window, my mouth watering. "Oh, they must taste so delicious," I said wistfully.

"And that poppy seed kalacs (kuchen) looks wonderful too," Grandmother sighed.

"Maybe this wasn't such a good idea," Grandfather said. "Now everyone is hungry for something they can not have!" He sounded very sad.

"But who is to say that you can not have a Napoleon or some of that poppy seed kuchen?" a voice behind us asked. A woman in a fur coat and hat took my hand. "Come on, let us all go into the bakery."

"Oh, no!" I protested, trying to pull my hand out of hers. But she wouldn't let go, and inside the bakery, bought a large Napoleon square, and some kuchen, just for us. "Froliche Weinachten," she called out merrily, and then disappeared into a crowd of people. A Christmas angel in a fur coat!

On the way back to the refugee camp, as I sank my teeth into that delicious, custard-filled Napoleon, and got powdered sugar all over myself, I was already happy. But there were more wonderful surprises ahead.

That evening, Christmas Eve, they lit the candles on the community Christmas tree, and all the adults came to watch our Christmas play, which went off very nicely. Everyone remembered their lines, and the choir sang some beautiful Hungarian Christmas songs. I noticed that people had tears in their eyes. Then the presents were handed out, for, yes indeed, there were presents for all the kids under that tree.

When I opened mine, I found a pair of red, fuzzy mittens and a matching scarf in the box, and inside one of the mittens, there was a little note, written in English. "Merry Christmas from Mary Anne, in Buffalo, New York, United States of America." Imagine that, a gift from a girl all the way in America! I wondered later how old she was, what she looked like, what she liked to do, as I tried to fall asleep while my imagination kept working overtime.

When I awoke on Christmas morning, it was already light out, and there were noises coming through the thin, wooden boards of the barrack.

"Good morning, sweetheart. Merry Christmas," Grandmother said.

"Why is there so much noise out there already?" I asked sleepily, rubbing my eyes.

"Well, I guess some early rising children are enjoying all the newly fallen snow."

"Oh, did it snow overnight?" I said, leaping from the cot and reaching for some warm clothes to put on. "How wonderful! And where is Grandfather?"

"He and some of the other men are shoveling some paths, so people can go for their breakfast, and to church."

Within seconds, I was out there too, marveling at nature's power to turn a drab refugee camp into a pristine, winter wonderland!

Soon, the surrounding, snow covered hills were filled with squealing Austrian children, sledding down those hills in their new Christmas sleds, or shushing down on their new skis, while refugee-camp children built snow men, had snowball fights, and made snow angels, squealing with just as much delight. Nature's gift of snow was free for everyone to enjoy!

Later as I gazed at the snow-covered mountains, with their majestic, snow-dusted spruce trees, so breathtakingly beautiful, my heart filled with joy, and with tears in my eyes, I thanked God for a wonderful Christmas. Even though we were far from home, we were surrounded by loved ones and the love and generosity of others—some perfect strangers. I knew it was a Christmas I would never forget.[2] ✳

CHRISTMAS CANDY CANE

History: The candy cane is a traditional American Christmas candy that is typically used to decorate the Christmas tree or is included in the stocking. Many stories surround the origin of the candy cane—all are religious and related to the night of the birth of the Christ child, Jesus. A popular story goes like this:

A candy maker in Indiana wanted to make a candy that would be a witness, so he made the Christmas candy cane. He incorporated several symbols for the birth, ministry, and death of Jesus Christ.

He began with a stick of pure white hard candy. White to symbolize the Virgin Birth and the sinless nature of Jesus, and hard to symbolize the Solid Rock, the foundation of the Church, and firmness of the promises of God.

The candy maker made the candy in the form of a *J* to represent the precious name of Jesus, who came to earth as our Savior. It could also represent the staff of the "Good Shepherd" with which He reaches down into the ditches of the world to lift out the fallen lambs who, like all sheep, have gone astray.

Thinking that the candy was somewhat plain, the candy maker stained it with red stripes. He used three small stripes to show the stripes of the scourging Jesus received by which we are healed. The large red stripe was for the blood shed by Christ on the cross so that we could have the promise of eternal life.

Unfortunately, the candy became known as a candy cane—a meaningless decoration seen at Christmastime. But the true meaning is still there for those who have eyes to see and ears to hear.

Christmas Idea:

Try these ideas for using candy canes:

- Use candy canes as stirring sticks for hot beverages.
- Add crushed candy canes to vanilla frosting and make sandwiches with cookies or graham crackers.
- Add crushed candy canes to cookies and treats.
- Melt chocolate bars or white almond bark, add crushed candy canes and chill.
- Sprinkle crushed candy canes on top of iced cupcakes or ice cream sundaes.
- Layer ice cream and hot fudge sauce with crushed candy canes and top with whipped cream for a peppermint twist treat.

Christmas Idea:

Make copies of the candy cane story, punch a hole in the top, and tie it with ribbon to the candy cane. Hand these out to family and friends as they visit, or dress up in Christmas costumes and take them to your neighbors. For smaller children, use this beautiful and simple rhyme titled "The Legend of the Candy Cane":

> *Look at the Candy Cane*
> *What do you see?*
> *Stripes that are red*
> *Like the blood shed for Me.*
> *White is for my Savior*
> *Who's sinless and pure!*
> *"J" is for Jesus, My Lord, that's for sure!*
> *Turn it around*
> *And a staff you will see.*
> *Jesus my shepherd*
> *Was born for Me!*

PORK LOIN ROAST

1 bone-in center pork loin roast, 4–6 pounds

2 Tbsp. olive oil

1/4 cup brandy

1/2 cup orange marmalade

2 tsp. fresh thyme

1 Tbsp. fresh parsley

1 Tbsp. Kosher salt

1 tsp. pepper

Preheat the oven to 375°F. Place the pork roast in a roasting pan with the rib bones facing up. Combine the oil, brandy, orange marmalade, and herbs and brush to cover the roast. Season the roast with salt and pepper. Cook the pork loin for 2 to 2 1/2 hours in the oven or until the meat registers 150°F on a thermometer. Let rest for 20 minutes before carving.

I Wonder as I Wander

Derived from an Appalachian folk song

I wonder as I wander out under the sky,
How Jesus, the Savior, did come forth to die;
For poor, ornery people like you and like I—
I wonder as I wander, out under the sky.

When Mary birthed Jesus, 'Twas in a cow's stall,
With wise men and farmers and shepherds and all.
But high from God's heaven a star's light did fall.
And the promise of ages it then did recall.

If Jesus had wanted for any wee thing,
A star in the sky or a bird on the wing;
Or all of God's angels in heaven to sing,
He surely could have had it, 'cause He was the King!

I wonder as I wander out under the sky,
How Jesus, the Savior, did come forth to die;
For poor, ornery people like you and like I—

I wonder as I wander, out under the sky.

Historical Note:

The early history of this carol is unknown. We do know that composer John Jacob Niles, while working in Appalachia as a surveyor, heard a girl singing three lines of a folk song and composed the remainder in 1933 from that inauspicious fragment.

LITTLE TREE

E. E. CUMMINGS

Little tree
little silent Christmas tree
you are so little
you are more like a flower.

who found you in the green forest
and were you very sorry to come away?
see I will comfort you
because you smell so sweetly

I will kiss your cool bark
and hug you safe and tight
just as your mother would
only don't be afraid

look the spangles
that sleep all the year in a dark box
dreaming of being taken out and allowed to shine,
the balls the chains red and gold the fluffy threads,

put up your little arms
and I'll give them all to you to hold
every finger shall have its ring
and there won't be a single place dark or unhappy

then when you're quite dressed
you'll stand in the window for everyone to see
and how they'll stare!
oh but you'll be very proud

and my little sister and I will take hands
and looking up at our beautiful tree
we'll dance and sing
"Noel Noel!"

Gift Idea for the Love of Your Life

Create a brag book for Christmas this year. Include photographs, newspaper articles of events your loved one was involved in, promotions at work, and any other accomplishments. (This could be something as simple as conquering a new pie recipe or hitting a hole-in-one.) Emphasize any volunteer work, personal victories (great or small), and anything else that makes you proud to be associated with that special person. Wrap it elegantly and present it in front of other people, where you can show it off and brag even more.

Christmas Gift Idea for the Elderly

The elderly are difficult to buy gifts for. They often don't want and certainly don't have room for a lot of "stuff." They also don't often have the strength, energy, or motivation to put up a tree each year. Delivering a small, live or artificial tree—already decorated—would be a great gift. Remember to show up to take it down after Christmas. Your elderly friend may not be able to do that alone.

Note: The elderly often have an artificial tree and decorations of their own, but aren't able to get the job done. Offer to do it for them. Bring cookies, eggnog, and a camera, and make it a family affair.

Christmas Dinner in Portugal

Traditional Portuguese Menu
Roast chicken, lamb, or turkey
Boiled codfish
Portuguese sprouts
Sonhos (pumpkin fritters)
Rice pudding with cinnamon
Bolo Rei (fruitcake)

The History
- Traditionally, Portuguese families gather for dinner or consoada on Christmas Eve. They enjoy a long, relaxed meal as they wait for Father Christmas. Some families set a place at the table in honor of their loved ones who have died.
- Consoada usually consists of boiled codfish and Portuguese sprouts cooked in pure olive oil. The main course is followed with a variety of desserts, including rice pudding with cinnamon, rabandas (similar to French toast), filhoses (fried desserts), broas de mel (pastries made with honey), and sonhos (pumpkin fritters).
- At midnight, most families attend a special Midnight Mass, called Missa do galo or "Rooster's Mass."
- On Christmas day, families visit with friends and enjoy a big lunch, normally with roast chicken, lamb, or turkey.

Did You Know?
- A favorite Christmas treat is turrón, a hard, white nougat with almonds.

- Another traditional dessert is the bolo rei, a wreath-like fruitcake laced with crystallized fruits and pine nuts.
- A broad bean (also known as a horse bean; looks like a very large lima bean) and a little present (usually a fake ring or a little doll) are baked inside the cake. The person who gets the piece of cake with the broad bean must pay for the next bolo rei.

For Our Portuguese Friends: Enjoy your Cepo de Natal. Traditionally, this oak Christmas log burns on the hearth throughout the day on Christmas.

The Perfect Bow

'Tis the season for bows on presents, bows on baskets, bows on wreaths, bows almost everywhere...but how do you make those beautiful, puffy bows?

The technique is simple—each time you complete a loop, you twist the ribbon one half turn around before you begin another loop so that the right side is always up. When your bow is as full as you like, wrap a wire around the center, twisting it to hold the loops in place.

Remember: always hold the center of the bow with your left hand and make new loops and twist with your right.

Did You Know?

Since 1966, the official White House Christmas tree, or the Blue Room Christmas Tree, has been donated by the National Christmas Tree Association.

December 6

KEEP CHRISTMAS
BEAUTIFUL

ANN SCHULTZ

Let us keep Christmas beautiful
Without a thought of greed,
That it might live forevermore
To fill our every need,
That it shall not be just a day,
But last a lifetime through,
The miracle of Christmastime
That brings God close to you.

A Newspaper Account of the First Electric Christmas Tree Lights

IN THE HOME OF EDWARD JOHNSON, NEW YORK CITY, 1882

*L*ast evening I walked over beyond Fifth Avenue and called at the residence of Edward H. Johnson, vice-president of Edison's electric company. There, at the rear of the beautiful parlors, was a large Christmas tree presenting a most picturesque and uncanny aspect. It was brilliantly lighted with many colored globes about as large as an English walnut and was turning some six times a minute on a little pine box. There were 80 lights in all encased in these dainty glass eggs, and about equally divided between white, red and blue. As the tree turned, the colors alternated, all the lamps going out and being relit at every revolution. The rest was a continuous twinkling of dancing colors, red, white, blue, white, red, blue—all evening.

I need not tell you that the scintillating evergreen was a pretty sight—one can hardly imagine anything prettier. The ceiling was crossed obliquely with two wires on which hung 28 more of the tiny lights; and all the lights and the fantastic tree itself with its starry fruit were kept going by the slight electric current brought from the main office on a filmy wire. The tree was kept revolving by a little hidden crank below the floor which was turned by electricity. It was a superb exhibition. ✷

Did You Know?

England has had only seven white Christmases in the entire twentieth century. Snow actually fell on Christmas Day just twice—1938 and 1976.

Bill for the Twelve Days of Christmas Gifts
From the Joyful Noiseletter

The complete catalog of gifts in the old Christmas carol "The Twelve Days of Christmas" today would cost you a total of $15,231.72! J. Patrick Bradley, chief economist at Provident National Bank in Philadelphia, figures the breakdown of prices for the 12 days as follows:

One partridge in a pear tree, $27.48 (Partridge, $15; pear tree, $12.48)

Two turtle doves, $50

Three French hens, $15

Four calling birds, $280

Five gold rings, $600

Six geese-a-laying, $150

Seven swans-a-swimming, $7,000

Nine ladies dancing, $2,417.90

Ten lords-a-leaping, $2,686.56

Eleven pipers piping, $947.70

Twelve drummers drumming, $1,026.68[3]

*The coming of Jesus into the world is
the most stupendous event in human history.*

Malcolm Muggeridge

Green Bean Casserole

2 cans green beans

1 can cream of mushroom soup

½ cup milk

Salt and pepper to taste

1 can cheddar French Fried Onions

Combine first four ingredients, then add half a can of French Fried Onions. Pour into a casserole dish. Crumble and sprinkle the remaining French Fried Onions over the top. Bake at 350°F for 30 minutes.

CHRISTMAS DINNER IN JAMAICA

Traditional Jamaican Menu
Ham
Oxtail
Curried goat
Rice and gungo peas

The History
- Christmas in Jamaica includes church services, candlelight ceremonies, concerts, all-night prayer meetings, and the singing of Christmas carols.
- The annual Christmas tree lighting ceremony in Kingston is a beloved tradition that involves the turning on of hundreds of colored bulbs on the tree, a fireworks display, caroling, and distribution of Christmas gifts to the poor.
- Christmas dinner is usually a big feast on Christmas Day.
- During the time of slavery, ham was cured by smoking it in large baskets called kring-kreng over a slow fire. Pimento was used to spice the meat. Since meat was scarce, this was an especially important Christmas tradition.
- The mothers of the family make a special Christmas pudding, using fruits that have been soaked in wine or rum for weeks in anticipation of the holidays.

Did You Know?
- A historical festival is performed at Christmastime. It was conceived as a festive opportunity given to the slave class by the planter class to celebrate Christmas—one of the few periods when the slaves were

relieved of their duties. Performers dance and act out their parts wearing flamboyant, brightly colored costumes to depict traditional characters.

- Sorrel, a popular and refreshing Christmas drink, is made by steeping red ripe berries in boiling water. It is sweetened with sugar and syrup and flavored with ginger, cloves, rum, or brandy and served over ice.

For Our Jamaican Friends: Although you live on an island that has never seen snow, and your houses have no chimneys, Santa Claus will definitely visit you, though he may arrive on a cart or donkey rather than a sleigh pulled by reindeer!

I stopped believing in Santa Claus when I was six.
Mother took me to see him in a department store and
he asked for my autograph.

SHIRLEY TEMPLE BLACK

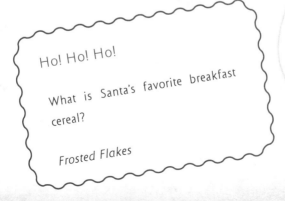

Ho! Ho! Ho!

What is Santa's favorite breakfast cereal?

Frosted Flakes

MY CHRISTMAS MIRACLE

TAYLOR CALDWELL

*F*or many of us, one Christmas stands out from all the others, the one when the meaning of the day shone clearest.

Although I did not guess it, my own truest Christmas began on a rainy spring day in the bleakest year of my life. Recently divorced, I was in my 20s, had no job, and was on my way downtown to go the rounds of the employment offices. I had no umbrella, for my old one had fallen apart, and I could not afford another one. I sat down in the streetcar, and there against the seat was a beautiful silk umbrella with a silver handle inlaid with gold and flecks of bright enamel. I had never seen anything so lovely.

I examined the handle and saw a name engraved among the golden scrolls. The usual procedure would have been to turn in the umbrella to the conductor, but on impulse I decided to take it with me and find the owner myself. I got off the streetcar in a downpour and thankfully opened the umbrella to protect myself. Then I searched a telephone book for the name on the umbrella and found it. I called, and a lady answered.

Yes, she said in surprise that was her umbrella which her parents, now dead, had given her for a birthday present. But, she added, it had been stolen from her locker at school (she was a teacher) more than a year before. She was so excited that I forgot I was looking for a job and went directly to her small house. She took the umbrella, and her eyes filled with tears.

The teacher wanted to give me a reward, but—though $20 was all I had in the world—her happiness at retrieving this special possession was such that to have accepted money would have spoiled something. We talked for a while, and I must have given her my address. I don't remember.

The next six months were wretched. I was able to obtain only temporary employment here and there, for a small salary, though this was what they now call the Roaring Twenties. But I put aside 25 or 50 cents when I could afford it for my little girl's Christmas presents. (It took me six months to save $8.) My last job ended the day before Christmas, my $30 rent was soon due, and I had $15 to my name—which Peggy and I would need for food. She was home from her convent boarding school and was excitedly looking forward to her gifts the next day, which I had already purchased. I had bought her a small tree, and we were going to decorate it that night.

The stormy air was full of the sound of Christmas merriment as I walked from the streetcar to my small apartment. Bells rang and children shouted in the bitter dusk of the evening, and windows were lighted and everyone was running and laughing. But there would be no Christmas for me, I knew, no gifts, no remembrance whatsoever. As I struggled through the snowdrifts, I just about reached the lowest point in my life. Unless a miracle happened I would be homeless in January, foodless, jobless. I had prayed steadily for weeks, and there had been no answer but this coldness and darkness, this harsh air, this abandonment. God and men had completely forgotten me. I felt old as death, and as lonely. What was to become of us?

I looked in my mailbox. There were only bills in it, a sheaf of them, and two white envelopes which I was sure contained more bills. I went up three dusty flights of stairs, and I cried, shivering in my thin coat. But I made myself smile so I could greet my little daughter with a pretense of happiness. She opened the door for me and threw herself in my arms, screaming joyously and demanding that we decorate the tree immediately.

Peggy was not yet six years old, and had been alone all day while I worked. She had set our kitchen table for our evening meal, proudly, and put pans out and the three cans of food which would be our dinner. For some reason, when I looked at those pans and cans, I felt broken-hearted. We would have only hamburgers for our Christmas dinner tomorrow, and gelatin. I stood in the cold little kitchen, and misery overwhelmed me. For the first time in my life, I doubted the existence of God and His mercy, and the coldness in my heart was colder than ice.

The doorbell rang, and Peggy ran fleetly to answer it, calling that it must be Santa Claus. Then I heard a man talking heartily to her and went to the door. He was a delivery man, and his arms were full of big parcels, and he was laughing at my child's frenzied joy and her dancing. This is a mistake, I said, but he read the name on the parcels, and they were for me. When he had gone I could only stare at the boxes. Peggy and I sat on the floor and opened them. A huge doll, three times the size of the one I had bought for her. Gloves. Candy. A beautiful leather purse. Incredible! I looked for the name of the sender. It was the teacher, the address simply California, where she had moved.

Our dinner that night was the most delicious I had ever eaten. I could only pray to myself, Thank You, Father. I forgot I had no money for the rent and only $15 in my purse and no job. My child and I ate and laughed together in happiness. Then we decorated the little tree and marveled at it. I put Peggy to bed and set up her gifts around the tree, and a sweet peace flooded me like a benediction. I had some hope again. I could even examine the sheaf of bills without cringing. Then I opened the two white envelopes. One contained a check for $30 from a company I had worked for briefly in the summer. It was, said a note, my Christmas bonus. My rent!

The other envelope was an offer of a permanent position with the government—to begin in two days after Christmas. I sat with the letter in my hand and the check on the table before me, and I think that was the most joyful moment of my life up to that time.

The church bells began to ring. I hurriedly looked at my child, who was sleeping blissfully, and ran down to the street. Everywhere people were walking to church to celebrate the birth of the Savior. People smiled at me, and

I smiled back. The storm had stopped; the sky was pure and glittering with stars.

The Lord is born! sang the bells to the crystal night and the laughing darkness. Someone began to sing, "Come, all ye faithful!"

I joined in and sang with the strangers all about me.

I am not alone at all, I thought. I was never alone at all.

And that, of course, is the message of Christmas. We are never alone. Not when the night is darkest, the wind coldest, the world seemingly most indifferent. For this is still the time God chooses. ✴

TAYLOR CALDWELL (1900–1985)

She wrote under the pen names Taylor Caldwell, Marcus Holland, and Max Reiner, but her real name was Janet Miriam Reback. A prolific American author of popular fiction, she often used real historical events or persons in her works. She was born in Manchester, England, into a family of Scottish background. Her family descended from the clan of MacGregor of which the Taylors are a subsidiary clan. In 1907, she emigrated to the United States with her family. At the age of eight, she started to write stories.

In 1931, she graduated from the University of Buffalo. In collaboration with her second husband, Marcus Reback, she wrote several bestsellers, the first of which was *Dynasty of Death*. As a writer, Caldwell was praised for her intricately plotted and suspenseful stories.

Caldwell continued writing until 1980, when a stroke left her deaf and unable to speak. She died in Greenwich, Connecticut, in September of 1985.

December 7

THE SHEPHERDS SING

GEORGE HERBERT

The shepherds sing; and shall I silent be?
My God, no hymn for Thee?
My soul's a shepherd too: a flock it feeds
Of thoughts, and words, and deeds.
The pasture is Thy word, the streams, Thy grace
Enriching all the place.
Shepherd and flock shall sing,
And all my powers out-sing the daylight hours.

"GOD JUL!"
(MERRY CHRISTMAS)

MARILYN JASKULKE

*G*randpa swung open the front door of his house in wintry, frigid Minnesota. I cringed at the squawk of compacted snow around the doorway. Mom, Dad, my younger brother, and I all hustled into the warmth of a Scandinavian Christmas Eve celebration.

"Kom in. Kom in," said Grandma in her Swedish brogue. In one fluid motion, she wiped her hands on her holiday apron and swept the silver-gray hair back from the temples of her face. As quickly as she spoke, she disappeared into the kitchen to complete the preparation of our Christmas Eve dinner.

Friends and relatives gathered yearly at my grandparents' Minnesota home for a gala celebration. It was common that adults chatted, at Christmastime, in their native Swedish, while the children spoke English, the only language we knew. The Christmas tree, with its sweeping boughs, stood in one corner of the living room. Each trinket brought memories of earlier years. I loved the shiny red Santa Claus bauble most of all. *I wonder what Santa will bring me this year? I hope I'll get new ice skates.* I could see my reflection in the Santa ornament and felt sure I'd been as good a little girl as I could have been for a six-year-old.

A string of blue and yellow Swedish paper flags floated among the tree branches, at Grandpa's insistence, a reminder of the origins of his family. Grandma's final touch in decorating the tree had been to drape thick angel hair around the branches. Red, green, yellow, and blue colored tree lights shimmered through the angel hair. They appeared as obscure distant faces of relatives who'd remained in the "old country," Sweden.

Always awed by the assortment of gifts under the tree, I pinched, poked, and peeped, hoping to find a package for me. When at last Grandpa stood in the doorway to the dining room and said, "Var sa god," we understood it was time to "come and get it."

Swedish meatballs, lingonberries, homemade Swedish limpa bread, potatoes, gravy, and vegetables filled our plates to overflowing. Grandpa boasted about the pickled herring. "Ya, ve vent downtown on da streetcar to da fish market. Ve bought da feesh and had ta bring it home on da streetcar vid us. Ya, it sure did smell. But Ma soaked da feesh and put vinegar and spices on it. It sure duz taste purty gud."

I slipped away from the table, crept behind the Christmas tree, pulled the lace curtains apart at the window, and peered into the darkness. *Santa may be out there. I sure wish they'd hurry up and get done eating.* Near the street light the world looked cold and white. No Santa waited outside. Flopping into Grandpa's wingback chair, I gazed around the familiar room. The crystal candy dish sat in its usual place, away from tiny fingers, but reachable now that I'd grown taller. I popped a Swedish mint into my mouth and began the long wait once more. The bright colors of the Oriental rug, as vivid as the lights on the Christmas tree, wove a pattern across the living room floor. Grandpa's sleek mahogany desk stood guard over the room. I listened for sounds from the other room, waiting for dinner to end.

With a final clatter of coffee cups, everyone began filtering into the living room and finding chairs to sit on. When Grandma appeared, minus her apron, I knew the time had come for gift giving. She grinned, found her flowered upholstered chair unoccupied and sat down. "Now ve can pass out da presents," she said.

Mom received her usual box of hankies and Lily of the Valley perfume. Dad opened a tie box. "I'll hang this in the closet with the others," he said.

Mom said something in Swedish and nudged Dad with her elbow.

My brother got a toy car, Grandma another copper pot for cooking, and

Grandpa a pocket watch. I watched as he proudly turned the gift from side to side, until a smile spread across his face. He loosened his vest pocket and carefully tucked the watch away, giving it a final pat. In one long stride, from his chair to the Christmas tree, Grandpa reached for a large package.

"Hmm, I vonder who dis is for?" He turned it upside down. He shook it with his strong hands. Stooping low to where I sat on the floor, he gave the big box to me.

I clasped my hands together and wondered which end of the box to open. Pulling the red ribbon off, I tore through the tissue paper and opened the box. *My Christmas wish has come true...my new ice skates! Santa must've arrived while we were eating and hidden the box under the tree.*

I held the skates in my arms like a precious prize, closed my eyes, and wished tomorrow would hurry and come. Then I would be skating round and round on the ice rink, my toes aching from the cold. But it didn't matter. I got what I had wished for—brand-new white figure skates!

Others opened their gifts, laughing, mixing Swedish with English and tossing wrapping paper and ribbons until the Oriental rug disappeared from sight. Then, as quickly as the clutter began—it ended. Paper, ribbons, gift tags, all vanished. Once again the room looked magical. The lights on the Christmas tree glistened, and the hidden faces behind the angel hair seemed to smile out at us, wishing us a "God Jul."

Beautiful strains of music began to float from Grandpa's violin, softly lulling us. Then suddenly, he broke in to a rousing dance tune, as though we needn't even think of dozing off. This was, after all, Christmas Eve.

Much later, bundled with coats, hats, scarves, and mittens, we headed into the frosty night. Clutched in my arms, new white figure skates, just my size, nestled in a box ready and waiting for their first morning on the ice.

"God Jul! Tack sa mycket," my grandparents said.

"Merry Christmas! Thank you very much," we all mimicked.

Our words hung like stars in the brisk night air. It was indeed, a very merry Christmas.[4] ✳

To us a Child is born, to us a Son is given; and the government shall be upon His shoulder, and His name shall be called Wonderful Counselor, Mighty God, Everlasting Father [of Eternity], Prince of Peace. Of the increase of His government and of peace there shall be no end, upon the throne of David and over his kingdom, to establish it and to uphold it with justice and with righteousness from the [latter] time forth, even forevermore. The zeal of the Lord of hosts will perform this.

(Isaiah 9:6–7, AMP)

Christmas Gift Idea for a Close Friend or Family Member

Think about giving a scrapbook of pictures of the two of you through the years. Add funny captions if you like, and put a note on the inside front telling that person how much you love them and what they mean to you.

Note: Be sure to use acid-free covers for your photographs.

Born on Christmas Day

1. Isaac Newton (1642)–English mathematician and physicist. Known as the "father of modern science."
2. Clara Barton (1821)—American Civil War nurse. Founder of the American National Red Cross.
3. Helena Rubinstein (1870)–Polish-born American philanthropist and cosmetician.
4. Conrad Hilton (1887)–American hotelier.
5. Humphrey Bogart (1889)–American actor who became a preeminent motion picture tough guy and was a top box-office attraction during the '40s and '50s.
6. Cab Calloway (1907)–American singer, drummer, and entertainer.
7. Anwar Sadat (1918)–Egyptian army officer. President of Egypt (1970–1981).
8. Jimmy Buffett (1946)–American singer and songwriter.
9. Rickey Henderson (1958)–Known as the greatest leadoff man in baseball history.
10. Alicia Keys (1981)–American rhythm and blues singer.

Died on Christmas Day

1. Yoshihito (1926)–Emperor of Japan
2. W. C. Fields (1946)–Comedian
3. Charlie Chaplin (1977)–American actor
4. Dean Martin (1995)–American actor

Handmade Gift Ideas

Baked goods, original poems, stories, paintings, help with yard work and other chores, and, of course, the Christmas gift favorite of every child in the '50s—the handwoven potholder!

Santa Stats

Average wage of a mall Santa: $11 an hour. With real beard: $20.

Office Notes for the Christmas Season

To: All Employees

From: Management

Effective immediately, employees should keep in mind the following guidelines in compliance with FROLIC (the Federal Revelry Office and Leisure Industry Council).

1. Running aluminum foil through the paper shredder to make tinsel is discouraged.
2. Work requests are not to be filed under "Bah humbug."
3. Company cars are not to be used to go over the river and through the woods to Grandma's house.
4. All fruitcake is to be eaten before July 25.
5. Eggnog will not be dispensed in vending machines.

The staff is encouraged to have a Happy Holiday.

CANDIED SWEET POTATOES

  6 large sweet potatoes
  $1/2$ cup butter
  2 cups white sugar
  1 tsp. ground cinnamon
  1 tsp. ground nutmeg
  1 tsp. vanilla extract
  Salt to taste

Peel the sweet potatoes and cut them into slices. Melt the butter or margarine in a heavy skillet and add the sliced sweet potatoes. Mix the sugar, cinnamon, nutmeg, and salt. Cover the sweet potatoes with sugar mixture and stir. Cover skillet, reduce heat to low, and cook for about 1 hour or until potatoes are "candied." They should be tender but a little hard around the edges. The sauce will turn dark. You will need to stir occasionally during the cooking. Stir in the vanilla just before serving. Serve hot.

CHRISTMAS TREES

History: In the seventh century a monk from Crediton, Devonshire, went to Germany to teach the Word of God. He did many good works there and spent much time in Thuringia, an area which was to become the cradle of the Christmas decoration industry.

Legend has it that he used the triangular shape of the fir tree to describe the Holy Trinity of God the Father, Son, and Holy Spirit. The converted people began to revere the fir tree as God's tree, as they had previously revered the oak. By the twelfth century it was being hung, upside down, from ceilings at Christmastime in central Europe as a symbol of Christianity.

The Christmas tree was introduced in the United States by German settlers and Hessian mercenaries paid to fight in the Revolutionary War. In 1804, U.S. soldiers stationed at Fort Dearborn in Chicago hauled trees from surrounding woods to their barracks.

The traditional Christmas tree has basically remained the same throughout the years. It is still any variety of pine tree, real or artificial, that is brought into the home and decorated. Typical tree decorations have included a variety of edible and homemade ornaments. Some of the earliest decorations included strings of cranberries or popcorn, glass baubles, candles, and paper ornaments in a variety of shapes and sizes.

Toward the end of the 1800s, another variation of the traditional Christmas tree appeared: the artificial Christmas tree. Artificial trees originated in Germany. Metal wire trees were covered with goose, turkey, ostrich, or swan feathers. The feathers were often dyed green to imitate pine needles.

In the 1930s, the Addis Brush Company created the first artificial-brush trees, using the same machinery that made their toilet brushes! The Addis "Silver Pine" tree was patented in 1950. The Christmas tree was designed to have a revolving light source under it, and colored gels allowed the light to shine in different shades as it revolved under the tree.

The Christmas tree carpet or skirt was inspired by the need to catch wax dripping on to the floor from the Christmas tree candles. By 1913, it was possible to purchase beautifully painted carpets. After electric lights became popular, it had become customary to place a white sheet under the tree to look like snow.

The Christmas tree is usually left up until New Year's Day.

Christmas Idea: Make decorating the tree its own special tradition. Take advantage of the family gathering on Thanksgiving Day to set up the artificial tree or go out and choose a live one. Allow family members—even the toddlers—to choose their own decorations and place them on the tree. If you can't do this on Thanksgiving Day, designate an evening in the weeks ahead to get together for the decorating of the tree. Placing the star on the top of the tree should go to the youngest family member present over the age of two. When the star is in place, the patriarch of the family turns on the lights.

Note: Enjoy yourself and don't expect the tree to look picture-perfect. You can always move things around later.

We rejoice in the light,
And we echo the song
That comes down through the night
From the heavenly throng.
Ay! we shout to the lovely evangel they bring,
An we greet in his cradle our Savior and King.

JOSIAH GILBERT HOLLAND

Tips for a Safe and Healthy Christmas Tree:

- Select the freshest-looking real tree available. Once home, make a fresh cut across the tree's base and immediately place it in water.
- Keep the tree's water container full at all times, checking the water level daily.
- Be extra careful with electricity, all open flames, and other heat sources during the holidays.
- Place the Christmas tree far away from heat registers, space heaters, fireplaces, and wood stoves.
- Regularly check the tree for dryness. If the needles fall off when you touch them or the stems break off when you bend them, your tree may be dry. Check the water level. If it is low, add water. If not, it's time to take down the tree.

SUGAR COOKIE ORNAMENTS

    1 batch sugar cookie dough (homemade or store
       bought)
    Christmas cookie cutters
    Drinking straw
    12" long dowel at least $3/16$" in diameter
    Ribbon

Roll out the cookie dough. Using cookie cutters, cut out different shapes. Use the drinking straw to poke a hole near the top of the cookie. (Make sure not to get too close to the edge of the cookie. To add holes to purchased cookies, heat a few at a time in a 300°F oven for about two minutes, then puncture cookie with drinking straw.) After baking, use the hole to attach ribbon and tie to anything. Tie to the tree and use as ornaments or use as package tie-ons.

To make a tree-topper star, roll cookie dough to about 3/8" thickness. Cut out the shape of a star, and working on a cookie sheet, press the star onto a 12"-long, 3/16" dowel. Bake the cookie, dowel and all, in a 350°F oven until lightly browned. Cool completely before lifting from the cookie sheet. The star may be left plain or decorated with icing. Wire the dowel to the top branch of the tree, and tie with a ribbon or clip on a bow.

December 8

*One of the most glorious messes in the world
is the mess created in the living room on Christmas day.
Don't clean it up too quickly.*

ANDY ROONEY

DAVID'S STAR OF BETHLEHEM

CHRISTINE WHITING PARMENTER

*S*cott Carson reached home in a bad humor. Nancy, slipping a telltale bit of red ribbon into her workbasket, realized this as soon as he came in.

It was the twenty-first of December, and a white Christmas was promised. Snow had been falling for hours, and in most of the houses wreaths were already in the windows. It was what one calls "a Christmasy-feeling day," yet, save for that red ribbon in Nancy's basket, there was no sign in the Carson home of the approaching festival.

Scott said, kissing her absentmindedly and slumping into a big chair, "This snow is the very limit. If the wind starts blowing there'll be a fierce time with the traffic. My train was twenty minutes late as it is, and—there's the bell. Who can it be at this hour? I want my dinner."

"I'll go to the door," said Nancy hurriedly, as he started up. "Selma's putting dinner on the table now." Relaxing into his chair Scott heard her open the front door, say something about the storm and, after a moment, wish someone a Merry Christmas.

A Merry Christmas! He wondered that she could say it so calmly. Three years ago on Christmas morning, they had lost their boy—swiftly—terribly, without warning. Meningitis, the doctor said. Only a few hours before the child had seemed a healthy, happy youngster, helping them trim the tree; hoping, with a twinkle in the brown eyes so like his mother's, that Santa Claus would remember the fact that he wanted skis! He had gone happily to bed after Nancy had read them "The Night Before Christmas," a custom of early childhood's days that the eleven-year-old lad still clung to. Later his mother remembered, with a pang, that when she kissed him good night he

91

had said his head felt "kind of funny." But she had left him light-heartedly enough and gone down to help Scott fill the stockings. Santa had not forgotten the skis; but Jimmy never saw them.

Three years—and the memory still hurt so much that the very thought of Christmas was agony to Scott Carson. Jimmy had slipped away just as the carolers stopped innocently beneath his window, their voices rising clear and penetrating on the dawn-sweet air:

"Silent night—holy night..."

Scott arose suddenly. He *must* not live over that time again. "Who was it?" he asked gruffly as Nancy joined him, and understanding the gruffness she answered tactfully, "Only the expressman."

"What'd he bring?"

"Just a—a package."

"One naturally supposes that," replied her husband, with a touch of sarcasm. Then, suspicion gripping him, he burst out, "Look here! If you've been getting a Christmas gift for me, I—I won't have it. I told you I wanted to forget Christmas. I—"

"I know, dear," she broke in hastily. "The package was only from Aunt Mary."

"Didn't you tell her we weren't keeping Christmas?" he demanded irritably.

"Yes, Scott; but—but you know Aunt Mary! Come now, dinner's on and I think it's a good one. You'll feel better after you eat."

But Scott found it unaccountably hard to eat; and later, when Nancy was reading aloud in an effort to soothe him, he could not follow. She had chosen something humorous and diverting; but in the midst of a paragraph he spoke, and she knew that he had not been listening.

"Nancy," he said, "is there any place—any place on God's earth where we can get away from Christmas?"

She looked up, answering with sweet gentleness, "It would be a hard place to find, Scott."

He faced her suddenly "I feel as if I couldn't stand it—the trees—the carols—the merrymaking, you know. Oh, if I could only sleep this week away! But...I've been thinking...would—would you consider for one moment going up to camp with me for a day or two? I'd go alone, but—"

"Alone!" she echoed. "Up there in the wilderness at Christmas time? Do you think I'd let you?"

"But it would be hard for you, dear, cold and uncomfortable. I'm a brute to ask it, and yet—"

Nancy was thinking rapidly. They could not escape Christmas, of course. No change of locality could make them forget the anniversary of the day that Jimmy went away. But she was worried about Scott, and the change of scene might help him over the difficult hours ahead. The camp, situated on the mountain a mile from any neighbors, would at least be isolated. There was plenty of bedding and a big fireplace. It was worth trying.

She said, cheerfully, "I'll go with you, dear. Perhaps the change will make things easier for both of us."

This was Tuesday, and on Thursday afternoon they stepped off the north-bound train and stood on the platform watching it vanish into the mountains. The day was crisp and cold. "Two above," the station master told them as they went into the box of a station and moved instinctively toward the red-hot "air-tight" stove which gave forth grateful warmth.

"I sent a telegram yesterday to Clem Hawkins, over on the mountain road," said Scott. "I know you don't deliver a message so far off; but I took a chance. Do you know if he got it?"

"Yep. Clem don't have a phone, but the boy come down for some groceries, and I sent it up. If I was you, though, I'd stay to the Central House. Seems as if it would be more cheerful—Christmas time."

"I guess we'll be comfortable enough if Hawkins airs out, and lights a fire," replied Scott, his face hardening at this innocent mention of the holiday. "Is there anyone around here who'll take us up? I'll pay well for it, of course."

"Ira Morse'll go; but you'll have to walk from Hawkinses. The road ain't dug out beyond...there's Ira now. You wait, an' I'll holler to him. Hey, Ira!" he called, going to the door, "Will you carry these folks up the Hawkinses? They'll pay for it."

Ira, a ruddy-faced young farmer, obligingly appeared, his gray work horse hitched to a one-seated sleigh of ancient and uncomfortable design.

"Have to sit three on a seat," he explained cheerfully; "but we'll be all the warmer for it. Tuck the buffalo robe 'round the lady's feet, mister, and you and me'll use the horse blanket. Want to stop to the store for provisions?"

"Yes. I brought some canned stuff, but we'll need other things," said Nancy. "I've made a list."

"Well, you got good courage," grinned the station master. "I hope you don't get froze to death up in the woods. Merry Christmas to yer, anyhow!"

"The same to you!" responded Nancy, smiling; and noted with a stab of pain that her husband's sensitive lips were trembling.

Under Ira's cheerful conversation, however, Scott relaxed. They talked of crops, the neighbors, and local politics—safe subjects all; but as they passed the district school, where a half-dozen sleighs or flivers were parked, the man explained: "Folks decoratin' the school for the doin's tomorrow afternoon. Christmas tree for the kids, and pieces spoke, and singin'. We got a real live schooma'am this year, believe *me*!"

They had reached the road that wound up the mountain toward the Hawkins farm, and as they plodded on, a sudden wind arose that cut their faces. Snow creaked under the runners, and as the sun sank behind the mountain Nancy shivered, not so much with cold as with a sense of loneliness and isolation. It was Scott's voice that roused her:

"Should we have brought snowshoes? I didn't realize that we couldn't be carried all the way."

"Guess you'll get there all right," said Ira. "Snow's packed hard as a drumhead, and it ain't likely to thaw yet a while. Here you are," as he drew up before the weather-beaten, unpainted farmhouse. "You better step inside a minute and warm up."

A shrewish-looking woman was already at the door, opening it but a crack, in order to keep out fresh air and cold.

"I think," said Nancy, with a glance at the deepening shadows, "that we'd better keep right on. I wonder if there's anybody here who'd help carry our bags and provisions."

"There ain't," answered the woman, stepping outside and pulling a faded gray sweater around her shoulders. "Clem's gone to East Conroy with the eggs, and Dave's up to the camp keepin' yer fire goin'. You can take the sled and carry yer stuff on that. There 'tis, by the gate. Dave'll bring it back when he comes. An' tell him to hurry. Like as not, Clem won't get back in time fer milkin'."

"I thought Dave was goin' to help Teacher decorate the school this afternoon," ventured Ira. He was unloading their things as he spoke and roping them to the sled.

"So'd he," responded the woman; "but there wa'n't no one else to light that fire, was they? Guess it won't hurt him none to work for his livin' like other folks. That new schoolma'am, she thinks o' nothing but—"

"Oh, look here!" said the young man, straightening up, a belligerent light in his blue eyes, "It's Christmas! Can Dave go back with me if I stop and milk for him? They'll be workin' all evenin'—lots o' fun for a kid like him, and—"

"No, he can't!" snapped the woman. "His head's enough turned now with speakin' pieces and singin' silly songs. You better be gettin' on, folks.

I can't stand here talkin' till mornin'."

She slammed the door, while Ira glared after her retreating figure, kicked the gate post to relieve his feelings, and then grinned sheepishly.

"Some grouch! Why, she didn't even ask you in to get warm! Well, I wouldn't loiter if I was you. And send that kid right back, or he'll get worse'n a tongue-lashin'. Well, good-bye to you, folks. Hope you have a merry Christmas."

The tramp up the mountain passed almost entirely in silence, for it took their united energy to drag the sled up that steep grade against the wind. Scott drew a breath of relief when they beheld the camp, a spiral of smoke rising from its big stone chimney like a welcome promise of warmth.

"Looks good, doesn't it? But it'll be dark before that boy gets home. I wonder how old—"

They stopped simultaneously as a clear, sweet voice sounded from within the cabin:

"Silent night...holy night..."

"My God!"

Scott's face went suddenly dead white. He threw out a hand as if to brush something away, but Nancy caught it in hers, pulling it close against her wildly beating heart.

"All is calm...all is bright."

The childish treble came weirdly from within, while Nancy cried, "Scott—dearest, don't let go! It's only the little boy singing the carols he's learned in school. Don't you see? Come! Pull yourself together. We must go in."

Even as she spoke the door swung open, and through blurred vision they beheld the figure of a boy standing on the threshold. He was a slim little boy with an old, oddly wistful face, and big brown eyes under a thatch of yellow hair.

"You the city folks that was comin' up? Here, I'll help carry in yer things."

Before either could protest he was down on his knees in the snow, untying Ira's knots with skillful fingers. He would have lifted the heavy suitcase himself, had not Scott, jerked back to the present by the boy's action, interfered.

"I'll carry that in." His voice sounded queer and shaky. "You take the basket. We're late, I'm afraid. You'd better hurry home before it gets too dark. Your mother said—"

"I don't mind the dark," said the boy quietly, as they went within. "I'll coast most o' the way down, anyhow. Guess you heard me singin' when you come along." He smiled, a shy, embarrassed smile as he explained: "It was a good chance to practice the Christmas carols. They won't let me, 'round home. We're goin' to have a show at the school tomorrow. I'm one o' the three kings—you know—'we three kings of Orient are.' I sing the first verse all by myself," he added with childish pride.

There followed a moment's silence. Nancy was fighting a desire to put her arms about the slim boyish figure, while Scott had turned away, unbuckling the straps of his suitcase with fumbling hands. Then Nancy said, "I'm afraid we've kept you from helping at the school this afternoon. I'm so sorry."

The boy drew a resigned breath that struck her as strangely unchildlike.

"You needn't to mind, ma'am. Maybe they wouldn't have let me go anyway; and I've got tomorrow to think about. I—I been reading one o' your books. I like to read."

"What book was it? Would you like to take it home with you for a—" She glanced at Scott, still on his knees by the suitcase, and finished hurriedly— "a Christmas gift?"

"Gee! Wouldn't I!" His wistful eyes brightened, then clouded. "Is there a place maybe where I could hide it 'round here? They don't like me to read much to home. They," (a hard look crept into his young eyes), "they burned up the book Teacher gave me a while back. It was *David Copperfield*, and I hadn't got it finished."

There came a crash as Scott, rising suddenly, upset a chair. The child jumped, and then laughed at himself for being startled.

"Look here, sonny," said Scott huskily, "you must be getting home. Can you bring us some milk tomorrow? I'll find a place to hide your book and tell you about it then. Haven't you got a warmer coat than this?"

He lifted a shabby jacket from the settle and held it out while the boy slipped into it.

"Thanks, mister," he said. "It's hard gettin' it on because it's tore inside. They's only one button," he added, as Scott groped for them. "She don't get much time to sew 'em on. I'll bring up the milk tomorrow mornin'. I got to hurry now or I'll get fits! Thanks for the book ma'am. I'd like it better'n anything. Good night."

Standing at the window Nancy watched him start out in the fast descending dusk. It hurt her to think of that lonely walk; but she thrust the thought aside and turned to Scott, who had lighted a fire on the hearth and seemed absorbed in the dancing flames.

"That's good!" she said cheerfully. "I'll get things started for supper, and then make the bed. I'm weary enough to turn in early. You might bring me the canned stuff in your suitcase, Scott. A hot soup ought to taste good tonight."

She took an apron from her bag and moved toward the tiny kitchen. Dave evidently knew how to build a fire. The stove lids were almost red, and the kettle was singing. Nancy went about her preparations deftly, tired though she was from the unaccustomed tramp, while Scott opened a can of soup, toasted some bread, and carried their meal on a tray to the settles before the hearthfire. It was all very cozy and "Christmasy," thought Nancy, with the wind blustering outside and the flames leaping up the chimney. But she was strangely quiet. The thought of that lonely little figure trudging off in the gray dusk persisted, despite her efforts to forget. It was Scott who spoke, saying out of a silence, "I wonder how old he is."

"The—the little boy?"

He nodded, and she answered gently, "He seemed no older than—I mean, he seemed very young to be milking cows and doing chores."

Again Scott nodded, and a moment passed before he said, "The work wouldn't hurt him though, if he were strong enough; but—did you notice, Nancy, he didn't look half fed? He is an intelligent little chap, though, and his voice—good lord!" he broke off suddenly. "How can a shrew like that bring such a child into the world? To burn his book! Nancy, I can't understand how things are ordered. Here's that poor boy struggling for development in an unhappy atmosphere—and our Jimmy, who had love, and understanding, and—tell me, why is it?"

She stretched out a tender hand; but the question remained unanswered, and the meal was finished in silence.

Dave did not come with the milk next morning. They waited till nearly noon, and then tramped off in the snow-clad, pine-scented woods. It was a glorious day, with diamonds sparkling on every fir tree, and they came back refreshed, and ravenous for the delayed meal. Scott wiped the dishes, whistling as he worked. It struck his wife that he hadn't whistled like that for months. Later, the last kitchen rites accomplished, she went to the window, where he stood gazing down the trail.

"He won't come now, Scott."

"The kid? It's not three yet, Nancy."

"But the party begins at four. I suppose everyone for miles around will be there. I wish—" she was about to add that she wished they could have gone too, but something in Scott's face stopped the words. She said instead, "Do you think we'd better go for the milk ourselves?"

"What's the use? They'll all be at the shindig, even that sour-faced woman, I suppose, but somehow—I feel worried about the boy. If he isn't here bright and early in the morning I'll go down and see what's happened. Looks as if it were clouding up again, doesn't it? Perhaps we'll get snowed in!"

Big, lazy-looking snowflakes were already beginning to drift down. Scott piled more wood on the fire, and stretched out on the settle for a nap. But Nancy was restless. She found herself standing repeatedly at the window looking at the snow. She was there when at last Scott stirred and wakened. He sat up blinking, and asked, noting the twilight, "How long have I been asleep?"

Nancy laughed, relieved to hear his voice after the long stillness.

"It's after five."

"Good thunder!" He arose, putting an arm across her shoulders. "Poor girl! I haven't been much company on this trip! But I didn't sleep well last night, couldn't get that boy out of my mind. Why, look!" Scott was staring out of the window into the growing dusk. "Here he is now! I thought you said—"

He was already at the door, flinging it wide in welcome as he went out to lift the box of milk jars from the sled. It seemed to Nancy, as the child stepped inside, that he looked subtly different—discouraged, she would have said of an older person; and when he raised his eyes she saw the unmistakable signs of recent tears.

"Oh, David!" she exclaimed, "why aren't you at the party?"

"I didn't go."

The boy seemed curiously to have withdrawn into himself. His answer was like a gentle "none of your business"; but Nancy was not without a knowledge of boy nature. She thought, "He's hurt—dreadfully. He's afraid to talk for fear he'll cry; but he'll feel better to get it off his mind." She said, drawing him toward the cheerful hearthfire, "But why not, Dave?"

He swallowed, pulling himself together with an heroic effort.

"I had ter milk. The folks have gone to Conroy to Gramma Hawkins's! I *like* Gramma Hawkins. She told 'em to be sure an' bring me; but there wasn't no one else ter milk, so...so..."

It was Scott who came to the rescue as David's voice failed suddenly.

"Are you telling us that your people have gone away, for *Christmas*, leaving you home alone?"

The boy nodded, winking back tears as he managed a pathetic smile.

"Oh, I wouldn't ha' minded so much if—if it hadn't been for the doin's at the school. Miss Mary was countin' on me ter sing, and speak a piece. I don't know who they could ha' got to be that wise man." His face hardened in a way not good to see in a little boy, and he burst out angrily, "Oh, I'd have gone—after they got off! *Darn 'em!* But they hung 'round till almost four, and—and then I went for my good suit they—they'd *hid* it—or carried it away!... And there was a Christmas tree..."

His voice faltered again, while Nancy found herself speechless before what she recognized as a devastating disappointment. She glanced at Scott, and was frightened at the consuming anger in his face; but he came forward calmly, laying a steady hand on the boy's shoulder. He said, and, knowing what the words cost him, Nancy's heart went out to her husband in adoring gratitude, "Buck up, old scout! We'll have a Christmas tree! And we'll have a party too, you and Mother and I—darned if we don't! You can speak your piece and sing your carols for us. And Mother will read us 'The'"—for an appreciable moment Scott's voice faltered, but he went on gamely—"'The Night Before Christmas.' Did you ever hear it? And I know some stunts that'll make your eyes shine. We'll have our party tomorrow, Christmas Day, sonny; but now" (he was stooping for his overshoes as he spoke), "now we'll go after that tree before it gets too dark! Come on, Mother. We want you, too!"

Mother! Scott hadn't called her that since Jimmy left them! Through tear-blinded eyes Nancy groped for her coat in the diminutive closet. Darkness was coming swiftly as they went into the snowy forest, but they found their tree, and stopped to cut fragrant green branches for decoration. Not till the tree stood proudly in its corner did they remember the lack of tinsel trimmings; but Scott brushed this aside as a mere nothing.

"We've got popcorn, and nothing's prettier. Give us a bite of supper, Nancy, and then I'm going to the village."

"The village! At this hour?"

"You take my sled, mister," cried David, and they saw that his eyes were happy once more, and child-like. "You can coast 'most all the way, like lightning! I'll pop the corn. I'd love to! Gee! It's lucky I milked before I come away!"

The hours that followed passed like magic to Nancy Carson. Veritable wonders were wrought in that small cabin; and oh, it was good to be planning and playing again with a little boy! Not till the child, who had been up since dawn, had dropped asleep on the settle from sheer weariness, did she add the finishing touches to the scene.

"It's like a picture of Christmas," she murmured happily. "The tree, so green and slender with its snowy trimmings—the cone-laden pine at the windows—the bulging stocking at the fireplace, and—and the sleeping boy. I wonder—"

She turned, startled by a step on the creaking snow outside, but it was Scott, of course. He came in quietly, not laden with bundles as she'd expected, but empty-handed. There was, she thought, a strange excitement in his manner as he glanced 'round the fire-lit room, his eyes resting for a moment on David's peaceful face. Then he saw the well-filled stocking at the mantel, and his eyes came back unswerving to hers.

"Nancy! Is—is it—?"

She drew nearer, and put her arms about him.

"Yes, dear, it's—Jimmy's—just as we filled it on Christmas Eve three years ago. You see, I couldn't quite bear to leave it behind us when we came away, lying there in his drawer so lonely—at Christmas time. Tell me you don't mind, Scott—won't you? We have our memories, but David—he has so little. That dreadful mother, and—"

Scott cleared his throat; swallowed, and said gently, "He has, I think, the loveliest mother in the world!"

"What do you mean?"

He drew her down onto the settle that faced the sleeping boy, and answered, "Listen, Nancy. I went to the schoolhouse. I thought perhaps they'd give me something to trim the tree. The party was over, but the teacher was there with Ira Morse, clearing things away. I told them about David—why he hadn't shown up; and asked some questions. Nancy—what do you think? That Hawkins woman isn't the child's mother! I *knew* it!

"Nobody around here ever saw her. She died when David was a baby, and his father, half crazed, the natives thought, with grief, brought the child here, and lived like a hermit on the mountain. He died when Dave was about six, and as no one claimed the youngster, and there was no orphan asylum within miles, he was sent to the poor farm, and stayed there until last year, when Clem Hawkins wanted a boy to help do chores, and Dave was the cheapest thing in sight. Guess you wonder where I've been all this time? Well, I've been interviewing the overseer of the poor farm—destroying red tape by the yard—resorting to bribery and corruption! But—hello, old man, did I wake you up?"

David, roused suddenly, rubbed his eyes. Then, spying the stocking, he wakened thoroughly and asked, "Say! Is—is it Christmas?"

Scott laughed, and glanced at his watch.

"It will be, in twelve minutes. Come here, sonny."

He drew the boy onto his knee, and went on quietly: "The stores were closed, David, when I reached the village. I couldn't buy you a Christmas gift, you see. But I thought if we gave you a *real mother*, and—and a father—"

"Oh, Scott!"

It was a cry of rapture from Nancy. She had, of course, suspected the ending to his story, but not until that moment had she let herself really believe it. Then, seeing the child's bewilderment, she explained, "He means, dear, that you're our boy now—for always."

David looked up, his brown eyes big with wonder.

"And I needn't go back to Hawkins's? Not *ever*?"

"Not ever," Scott promised, while his throat tightened at the relief in the boy's voice.

"And I'll have folks, same as the other kids?"

"You've guessed right." The new father spoke lightly in an effort to conceal his feeling. "That is, if you think we'll do!" he added, smiling.

"Oh, you'll—"

Suddenly inarticulate, David turned, throwing his thin arms around Scott's neck in a strangling, boylike hug. Then, a bit ashamed because such things were new to him, he slipped away, standing with his back to them at the window, trying, they saw with understanding hearts, to visualize this unbelievable thing that had come, a miracle, into his starved life. When after a silence they joined him, the candle on the table flared up for a protesting moment, and then went out. Only starlight and firelight lit the cabin now; and Nancy, peering into the night, said gently, "How beautifully it has cleared! I think I never saw the stars so bright."

"Christmas stars," Scott reminded her and, knowing the memory that brought the roughness to his voice, she caught and clasped his hand.

It was David who spoke next. He was leaning close to the window, his elbows resting on the sill, his face supped in his two hands. He seemed to have forgotten them as he said, dreamily, "It's Christmas...silent night...holy night...like the son. I wonder—"

He looked up trustfully into the faces above him. "I wonder if—if maybe one of them stars isn't the Star of Bethlehem!" ✴

CHRISTMAS BELLS

ELLA WHEELER WILCOX

When Christmas bells are swinging
Above the fields of snow,
We hear sweet voices ringing
From lands of long ago,
And etched on vacant places
Are half-forgotten faces
Of friends we used to cherish,
And loves we used to know.

Christmas renews our youth by stirring our wonder.
The capacity for wonder has been called our most pregnant human
faculty, for in it are born our art, our science, our religion.

RALPH SOCKMAN

Adeste Fideles
(O Come All Ye Faithful)

Written by John Francis Wade
Translated from Latin into English by Frederick Oakeley

O come all ye faithful, joyful and triumphant,
O come ye, O come ye, to Bethlehem!
Come and behold Him, born the King of angels!
O come, let us adore Him,
O come, let us adore Him,
O come, let us adore Him,
Christ the Lord!

Sing, choirs of angels, sing in exultation,
O sing, all ye citizens of heaven above!
Glory to God, glory in the highest!
O come, let us adore Him,
O come, let us adore Him,
O come, let us adore Him,
Christ the Lord!

Yea, Lord, we greet Thee, born this happy morning.
Jesus, to Thee be all glory giv'n;
Word of the Father, now in flesh appearing!
O come, let us adore Him,
O come, let us adore Him,
O come, let us adore Him,
Christ the Lord!

"Adeste Fideles" was written around 1743 by Englishman John Francis Wade, a Catholic layman and music teacher. In 1841, Frederick Oakeley translated it into English. In 1852, he again translated the hymn into the English words we know today as "O Come, All Ye Faithful."

A BABE IS BORN IN BETHLEHEM

Author Unknown

A Babe is born in Bethlehem, Bethlehem,

Therefore rejoice Jerusalem,

Hallelujah! Hallelujah!

Within a manger He doth lie, He doth lie,

Whose throne is set above the sky.

Hallelujah! Hallelujah!

Stillness was all the manger round, manger round,

The creature its Creator found.

Hallelujah! Hallelujah!

The wise men came, led by the star, by the star,

Gold, myrrh, and incense brought from far.

Hallelujah! Hallelujah!

His mother is the virgin mild, virgin mild,

And He the Father's only Child.

Hallelujah! Hallelujah!

December 9

What a blessing Christmas is! What it does for friendship! Why, if there were no Christmas...we'd have to invent one, for it is the one season of the year when we can lay aside all gnawing worry, indulge in sentiment without censure, assume the carefree faith of childhood, and just plain "have fun." Whether they call it Yuletide, Noel, Weihnachten, or Christmas, people around the earth thirst for its refreshment as the desert traveler for the oasis.

D. D. MONROE

A Bed in My Heart

MARTIN LUTHER

Ah, dearest Jesus, holy Child,
Make Thee a bed soft, undefiled,
Within my heart, that it may be
A quiet chamber kept for Thee.
My heart for very joy doth leap,
My lips no more can silence keep.
I too must sing, with joyful tongue,
That sweetest ancient cradle song,
Glory to God in highest Heaven,
Who unto man His Son hath given,
While angels sing with pious mirth,
A glad New Year to all the earth.

*Christmas is a day of meaning and traditions,
a special day spent in the warm circle of
family and friends.*

MARGARET THATCHER

TOP TEN CHRISTMAS SONGS
OF ALL TIME

1. "All I Want for Christmas Is My Two Front Teeth"
   (Donald Gardner) Spike Jones—1948. Also recorded by: Joanie Bartels; Boston Pops Orchestra; The Chipmunks; Nat King Cole; Harry Connick Jr.; The Countdown Kids; Dan Crow; Do-Re-Mi Children's Chorus; Dread Zeppelin; Hampton String Quartet; Oliver Jones; Sammy Kaye; Luther Kent/Trick Bag; Kuh Ledesma; Jerry Nelson; New Black Eagle Jazz Band; The Platters; George Rock; George Strait; and Tiny Tim.

2. "Deck the Halls" (Traditional)
   Julie Andrews—1968; Herbie Hancock & Chick Corea—1969; John Denver & The Muppets—1979. Also recorded by: Nat King Cole; Connie Brown; Lorie Line; Placido Domingo; Dick Haymes; Mario Lanza; The Chipmunks; The Lettermen; Roger Williams; Willie Nelson; Sons of the San Joaquin; The Platters.

3. "Frosty the Snowman"
   (Steve Nelson / Jack Rollins); Gene Autry & The Cass County Boys—1950; Nat King Cole & The Singing Pussy Cats—1950; Guy Lombardo & His Royal Canadians (vocal Kenny Gardner)—1950; Perry Como—1953; The Ronettes—1963; Willie Nelson—1979; Glen Campbell—1992. Also recorded by: Bing Crosby; Loretta Lynn; The Chipmunks; Wayne Newton; Ray Conniff; Fats Domino; Beach Boys; Spike Jones; Andy Williams; George Strait; Ella Fitzgerald; Glenn Miller; Hank Snow.

4. "I Saw Mommy Kissing Santa Claus"
   (T. Connor); Jimmy Boyd—1952; Molly Bee—1952; Spike Jones & His City Slickers (vocal: George Rock)—1952; The Beverley Sisters—1953; Billy Cotton & His Band (vocals: The Mill Girls & The Bandits)—1953. Also recorded by: Andy Williams; The Jackson 5; Bobby Helms; The Drifters; Perry Como; The Four Seasons; Daniel O'Donnell; The Platters; The Ronettes; Dion; Jane Krakowski; John Prine; Tiny Tim; Rosie O'Donnell; Vince Charles.

5. "I'll be Home for Christmas"

(Kim Gannon / Walter Kent / Buck Ram); Bing Crosby & The John Scott Trotter Orchestra—1943; Perry Como (with Mitchell Ayres' Orchestra)—1946; Elvis Presley—1957; Frank Sinatra—1957; Johnny Mathis—1958; Frankie Avalon—1962; The Carpenters—1978; Anne Murray—1981; Barbara Mandrell—1984; Lee Greenwood—1987; Jack Jones—1987; Vince Gill—1994. Also recorded by: Ron Dante; Dean Martin; Lou Rawls; John Berry; Oak Ridge Boys; Al Green; Jim Nabors; Beach Boys; Mickey Gilley; Harry Connick Jr.

6. "Here Comes Santa Claus"

(Gene Autry/Oakley Haldeman); Gene Autry—1947; Bing Crosby—1950; Spike Jones—1956; Elvis Presley—1957; Ray Conniff—1959; Ramsey Lewis—1960; Bob B. Soxx & The Blue Jeans—1963; Willie Nelson—1979; Dwight Yoakam—1997. Also recorded by: Asleep at the Wheel; The Platters; Doris Day; Eddy Arnold; Glen Campbell; Carmen Cavallaro; Kitty Wells; Bobby Helms; The Andrews Sisters; Pat Boone.

7. "Jingle Bells"

(James Pierpoint—1857); Recorded on Edison Cylinder by the Edison Male Quartette—1898; Hayden Quartet—1902; Benny Goodman—1936; Glenn Miller—1941; Bing Crosby and the Andrews Sisters—1943 (popularized the song); Les Paul—1961

8. "Santa Claus Is Coming to Town"

(Fred Coots/Haven Gillespie); Frank Sinatra—1947; Bobby Helms—1958; Eddy Arnold—1961; The Crystals—1963; The Four Seasons—1966; Tony Bennett—1968; Neil Diamond—1992; Frank Sinatra & Cyndi Lauper—1992; Michael Bolton—1996. Also recorded by: Gene Autry; The Andrews Sisters; Pat Boone; Paul Anka; Mariah Carey; Bing Crosby; Ron Dante; Dion; The Drifters; Judy Garland; Vince Gill; Al Hirt; The Carpenters; Glen Campbell; Judy Collins; The Beach Boys; Ray Charles; Nat King Cole; Burl Ives; Bob Hope; Perry Como; Johnny Mathis; Brenda Lee; Bert Kaempfert; Peggy Lee; Patti LaBelle; Don McLean; Daniel O'Donnell; Wayne Newton; Glenn Miller; Lou Rawls; The Supremes; Jimmy Rosselli; Smokey Robinson; Bobby Vinton; Andy Williams; Bryan White; The Temptations; Jerry Jeff Walker; George Strait; Randy Travis; Oak Ridge Boys; The Platters.

9. "Rudolph, the Red-Nosed Reindeer"

(Johnny Marks); Gene Autry & The Pinafores—1949; Spike Jones & His City Slickers—1950; Bing Crosby—1950; Burl Ives—1952; Perry Como—1959; Ray Conniff Singers—1959; Ella Fitzgerald—1960; The Chipmunks—1960; The Platters—1963; The Crystals—1963; Johnny Mathis—1963; Dean Martin—1965; The Supremes—1965; Pat Boone—1966; Lena Horne—1966; Ferlin Husky—1967; The Jackson 5—1970; The Temptations—1970; John Denver—1975; Merle Haggard—1978; Willie Nelson—1979; Dolly Parton—1990; Harry Connick Jr.—1993; Alan Jackson—1996; George Strait—1999; Suzy Bogguss—2003. Also recorded by: Bellamy Brothers; Rosemary Clooney; Tony Bennett; Neil Diamond; Moe Bandy; Lynn Anderson; Fats Domino; Crystal Gayle; Ray Charles; Clint Black; Red Foley; Foster & Allen; Bobby Helms; Hank Locklin; Patti Page; Lynyrd Skynyrd; Jimmy Roselli; Hank Snow; Hank Thompson; B. J. Thomas; Jerry Jeff Walker; Dion; Texas Tornados; Keely Smith; Conway Twitty; Ventures; Jimmy Wakely; Aaron Tippin: Mitch Miller; Don McLean; Chris Isaak; Skeeter Davis; Helen Reddy; Sammy Kaye; Freddy Cannon; Paul Anka; and many others.

10. "The Twelve Days of Christmas"

(Traditional) Recorded too many times to count, often as a parody. Notable examples: Allan Sherman—1963; John Denver and the Muppets—1979; and Natalie Cole—1998.

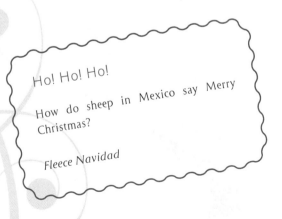

Ho! Ho! Ho!

How do sheep in Mexico say Merry Christmas?

Fleece Navidad

CHRISTMAS DINNER IN DENMARK

Traditional Danish Menu
Roast duck
Potatoes and gravy
Cooked cabbage
Rice pudding with cherry sauce

The History

- The main Christmas celebration is held on Christmas Eve, but the day before, December 23, is called Little Christmas Eve or lille juleaften. Families decorate the tree with colored glass balls and little red men (Santa's helpers, called nisser), and homemade hearts with raisins and nuts inside. Some families still put candles on the tree, but most use Christmas lights. A star goes on the top.

- Risengrod (rice boiled with milk and cinnamon) is eaten for dinner on Little Christmas Eve and some is left out for Santa's helpers.

- Guests arrive on Christmas Eve and are served cookies, hot chocolate, and glögg. Presents are placed under the tree.

- Dinner is served at dark (around 4 p.m.) and usually consists of roast pork or duck with crackling, stewed red cabbage, and small boiled potatoes fried in butter and sugar. Dessert consists of rice pudding with chopped almonds and whipped cream.

Did You Know?

- A whole almond is hidden in the pudding and whoever gets the almond receives the almond present, traditionally a marzipan pig.

- Glögg is the traditional Christmas drink. It is a mulled wine beverage made with red wines, Muscatel, Aquavit and spiced with orange, cinnamon, cardamom, and cloves. It is served hot over plump raisins and blanched skinned almonds after dinner.

- Crackling refers to the skin of the duck, which is drizzled with wine vinegar or cold water to make it crisp and crackly.

For Our Danish Friends: It's time for the children to get out their Christmas calendars! These are made of paper and filled with chocolate hidden behind twenty-four small windows, allowing one piece each day until December 24. Some have small pictures behind the windows, and others are embroidered with little gifts tied to them.

Gift Idea for the Man in Your Life
Sometimes the best gift for a guy is to see that you enjoy what he enjoys. If he has a passion for sports, buy him two tickets to see his favorite team play and then go along, even if sports are hardly your cup of tea. If he loves music, concert tickets might be more suitable. Give him the gift of entertainment and the gift of time together.
Santa Claus has the right idea.

Roasted Chestnuts

6 cups whole chestnuts

Using a paring knife, cut an *X* on the flat side of each nut, being sure to cut through the skin. This process is also called scoring. Roast the chestnuts by spreading them in a single layer on a cookie sheet and cooking at 425°F for 15–20 minutes, stirring occasionally to avoid any hot spots. Remove the chestnuts from the oven and peel while they're still warm. If they are too warm to handle, consider using a clean cotton towel to help remove the skins.

CHRISTMAS LIGHTS

History: It is believed that Martin Luther, the Protestant reformer, was the first to add lighted candles to his Christmas tree. He was so taken with the Christmas night sky that he wished to bring "the lights of the stars" into the home of his family. Candles for the tree were glued with melted wax to a tree branch or attached by pins. Around 1890, candle-holders were first used. Between 1902 and 1914, small lanterns and glass balls to hold the candles started to be used.

In 1882, the first Christmas tree was lit by the use of electricity. Edward Johnson—an inventor who worked under the direction of Thomas Edison—lighted up a Christmas tree in New York City with eighty small electric light bulbs. His little Christmas invention was soon being mass produced. A decade later, they were being used by department stores in their Christmas displays.

The long and beloved tradition of lighting the national Christmas tree began in 1923, when Calvin Coolidge ceremoniously lit the first outdoor tree at the White House.

An entire industry has grown up from those humble beginnings. Simple strands of Christmas tree lights are now just a starting point in the use of Christmas lights. Since the 1950s it has been common for individuals to decorate outdoors as well. It's now common to see lights strung along eaves, wound around shrubs, woven through the branches of trees, and outlining all types of large lawn ornaments. Many outdoor light shows have become so extravagant, most sporting flashing lights and sound effects, that neighbors complain. Lines of cars weave through the neighborhoods looking at the displays.

Christmas Idea: Create an Advent Wreath. This is a Lutheran custom that originated in Eastern Germany. It should be round at the base as a symbol of God's eternity and mercy, of which every season of Advent is a new reminder; and it is made of evergreens to symbolize God's "ever-lastingness" and our immortality. Green is also the Church's color of hope and new life. Four candles, three purple or violet that represent penance, sorrow, and longing expectation, and one rose or pink that represents the hope and coming joy, are placed within to represent the four weeks of Advent. They are replaced with white candles for the Christmas season which ends with Epiphany.

Some families place their Advent wreath on the dinner table every evening through the season of Advent and eat by its light. On the first week, the single candle seems very feeble and lonely, which might remind the family of the faithful all over the world who are living in isolation or hostility. On the second week, there are two lights, which might remind the family that where two or more are gathered in Christ's name, He is present. On the third week, the pink candle is lit, reminding the family of the Holy Trinity. Finally, all four candles are lit.

Christmas Idea: A wonderful Canadian custom calls for a candelabra with twenty-five small candles surrounding one large candle. The small candles are lit for loved ones and the central candle for Jesus. Once the center candle is lit, the Happy Birthday song is sung for baby Jesus.

Christmas Idea: Luminarias or farolitos—popular in the Southwest U.S. and Mexico—are easy to make and add beauty to your Christmas celebration. You will need paper sacks, sand, and votive candles.

Fill the bottom of each paper bag with about two inches of sand. Place a small, votive candle in the center and press it into the sand. Add several small stones to weigh down the bag. Light the candle with a long-nozzled lighter.

You can make them even more decorative by stenciling Christmas patterns on the front of your bags. Cut out the patterns and tape colored crepe paper inside the bags.

Note: These are too dangerous to keep indoors. They look wonderful on the patio or outlining the driveway.

Tips for Safe Christmas Lights:

- Check all Christmas tree lights, other electric decorations, and electrical appliances for wear (frayed cords, etc.). Do not use lights, decorations, or appliances with worn electrical cords. Use only UL-approved electrical decorations and extension cords.
- Unplug tree lights and other decorations when out of the room or while sleeping.

Ho! Ho! Ho!

Christmas is just plain weird. What other time of the year do you sit in front of a dead tree in your living room eating candy and snacks out of your socks?

PINE CONE DOOR DECORATION

You will need:

Several large pine cones

5 yards of weather-resistant velvet ribbon (3"-wide)

Floral wire

Make a large bow with the ribbon, catching the loops at the center with a length of floral wire. Also at the center, attach long ribbon streamers with another length of wire. Bend the ends of both wires into a loop for hanging. Clip the ends of the streamers into an attractive notched shape.

Wrap a piece of floral wire around the base of several pine cones, twisting these wires around each streamer.

Project tip:

Clean your cones with a stiff brush to remove dirt. Place any cones that are sticky in a 200°F oven for a few minutes. After the cones have cooled, rinse them and dry thoroughly.

Silent Night!

Joseph Mohr

Silent night, holy night
All is calm, all is bright
Round yon Virgin Mother and Child
Holy Infant so tender and mild
Sleep in heavenly peace
Sleep in heavenly peace.

Silent night, holy night!
Shepherds quake at the sight
Glories stream from heaven afar
Heavenly hosts sing Alleluia!
Christ, the Saviour is born

Christ, the Saviour is born.

Silent night, holy night
Son of God, love's pure light
Radiant beams from Thy holy face
With the dawn of redeeming grace
Jesus, Lord, at Thy birth
Jesus, Lord, at Thy birth

HISTORICAL NOTE:

The original six stanzas of this beloved Christmas hymn were written by a young priest assigned to a church in Mariapfarr, Austria. One common story concerning why Mohr wrote the poem states that mice destroyed the bellows of the church organ, disabling it on the day before the Christmas service. In response the priest quickly wrote a song that he felt could be accompanied by guitar. He took the poem to his friend, musician-school-teacher Franz Gruber who lived nearby and asked him to compose a melody for the piece. Mohr's real reason for writing the song is unknown. What can be confirmed is that the two men sang the song "Stille Nacht! Heilige Nacht!" for the first time that evening in front of the altar in St. Nicholas Church.

An organ builder and repairman obtained a copy of the song when he visited St. Nicholas church, giving it a wider audience. The song was then adopted by two traveling families of folk singers, much like the Trapp Family Singers. Their version became the carol we know today. The hymn's American debut was at the Alexander Hamilton Monument outside Trinity Church in New York City.

SKATING AT RATZEBURG

TAKEN FROM "CHRISTMAS OUT OF DOORS" BY SAMUEL TAYLOR COLERIDGE

The lower lake is now all alive with skaters, and with ladies driven onward by them in their ice cars. Mercury, surely, was the first maker of skates, and the wings at his feet are symbols of the invention.

In skating there are three pleasing circumstances: the infinitely subtle particles of ice which the skate cuts up, and which creep and run before the skate like a low mist, and in sunrise or sunset become coloured; second, the shadow of the skater in the water, seen through the transparent ice; and third, the melancholy undulating sound from the skate, not without variety; and when very many are skating together, the sounds and the noises give an impulse to the icy trees, and the woods all round the lake tinkle. ✶

December 10

WHAT MAKES CHRISTMAS?

AUTHOR UNKNOWN

"What makes Christmas?"
I asked my soul,
And this answer came back to me:
"It is the Glory of heaven
Come down in the hearts of humanity—
Come in the spirit and heart of a Child,
And it matters not what we share
At Christmas; it isn't Christmas at all
Unless the Christ child be there."

THE TINIEST MIRACLE

BONNIE COMPTON HANSON

"The Year of the Big Nothing"—that's what I called the Christmas I turned thirteen.

We did have a Christmas tree. As usual, we kids helped Daddy find one up in our forest and bring it back to our modest little farmhouse. We covered it with homemade decorations and popcorn garland, then wrapped up some of our pencil-and-crayon "masterpieces" to put underneath for each other.

But that was it for gifts; we had money for nothing else. *Nada. Zilch.* There was nothing for Christmas dinner except homemade pinto bean soup and cornbread, with some of Mother's home-canned pickles. Oh yes, there were also the nuts and apples we'd gathered ourselves in the fall.

On Christmas Eve, hearing my father read us the story of the First Noel out of the old family Bible gave me warm, fuzzy goosebumps. But still I felt very sad. We'd always had presents of one kind or another—dolls, bicycles, games, *something*. Always!

I thought of all the wonderful treasures we kids had drooled over in the Sears "wish book." We'd touched the shiny pages of the catalog as if they were jewels. Dolls! Bikes! Board games! Books! Stuffed animals! Costume jewelry! Coats, caps, new shoes! Proper mittens knit from wool, instead of make-do ones cut out of old blankets! So much to drool over—couldn't just one of them be for us?

Then I had a thought. If God could create an awesome miracle such as the birth of Baby Jesus, couldn't He create a small one just for us, just for this one day? Even just a teeny-tiny one? If not for my older sister, Betty, and me, couldn't there at least be a miracle for the younger ones?

"Please, dear God," I prayed, "I know it's probably impossible, but could

You please bring us some Christmas gifts this year? Or at least something wonderful to eat— You know, like in the old times before we got so poor?"

I didn't even want to get up that Christmas morning and face the empty tree. Instead, my older sister and I huddled under the covers, trying to postpone the inevitable. Till—

"Betty, Bonnie, wake up!" cried our younger sister and brothers. "Come see what Santa brought!"

With whoops of joy, they pulled us out of bed and into the living room. Sure enough, a pile of packages—brightly wrapped with Sunday funnies and tissue paper (carefully saved from previous years) and tied with string—glowed beneath our tree.

"Mommy! Daddy! Santa's been here! Can we open our presents now, pretty please?"

Not just presents, but treasures they were, all made by our parents. Despite working all day as a teacher and running a farm in the evenings, Mother had obviously stayed up long after we had gone to bed each night sewing new dresses for us girls, shirts and pajamas for my brothers, even a cuddly rag doll for little Paula—all out of gaily printed feed and flour sacks. And Daddy had made a toy truck for Bobby out of scrap lumber. They had also thoughtfully stuffed our stockings full of the nuts and apples we'd collected ourselves in the fall.

So, God did answer my prayer for a tiny miracle after all. Or at least He had just started to. For later in the day, one of our uncles drove up with a trunk full of food, including candy, oranges, lemons, and dates—even a chicken all ready to cook, bags of flour and sugar, and lots of potatoes and carrots and cabbage.

And then another uncle and his girlfriend came by to see us, bringing more candy, shiny new toys for the little ones, and even some clothes and costume jewelry for us older girls. They were his girlfriend's discards, to be

124

sure—but new and sparkly and glamorous to us. I could hardly wait until Christmas vacation was over and I could show them off at school!

Mother, delighted with her treasures, couldn't get to the kitchen fast enough, and my older sister and I followed close behind, eager to help (and taste!). Not long afterward, we were all sitting down to steaming platefuls of fried chicken, mashed potatoes and gravy, home-canned corn and pickles, Mother's famous lemon meringue pie—plus hot bean soup and cornbread and coleslaw. Enough for us, all our company, and leftovers too. Even scraps for our blissful dog!

No, the presents we received that Christmas weren't the ones we had dreamed of—not the shiny new "wish book" kind. But they were enough to help me realize that God still answers prayer and that even His teeniest-tiniest miracles are giant-sized—especially at Christmas![5] ✳

Gift Ideas for the Environmentalist in Your Life

Low-flow shower heads, rechargeable flashlights, fire extinguishers, tickets to a play, and BOOKS!

Blessed is the season which
engages the whole world in a conspiracy of love.

HAMILTON WRIGHT MABIE

Then a shoot will spring from the stem of Jesse,
And a branch from his roots will bear fruit.
And the Spirit of the LORD will rest on Him,
The spirit of wisdom and understanding,
The spirit of counsel and strength,
The spirit of knowledge and the fear of the LORD.
And He will delight in the fear of the LORD,
And He will not judge by what His eyes see,
Nor make a decision by what His ears hear;
But with righteousness He will judge the poor,
And decide with fairness for the afflicted of the earth;
And He will strike the earth with the rod of His mouth,
And with the breath of His lips He will slay the wicked.

(Isaiah 11:1–4, NASB)

Did You Know?

In England two hundred years ago, turkeys were walked to market in herds. They wore booties to protect their feet.

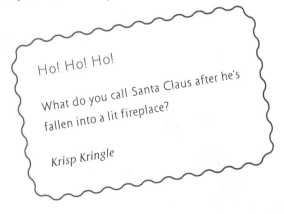

Ho! Ho! Ho!

What do you call Santa Claus after he's fallen into a lit fireplace?

Krisp Kringle

BREAD PUDDING

3 eggs

1 cup sugar

2 tsp. vanilla extract

1 tsp. ground cinnamon

1 tsp. ground nutmeg

1/4 cup unsalted butter, melted

2 cups low fat milk

6 slices sourdough bread

1/2 cup raisins

1/2 cup chopped pecans

2 cups low-fat vanilla frozen yogurt

Beat eggs in an electric mixer on high speed until frothy. Add next 5 ingredients. Continue beating on a lower speed while adding milk. Cut bread slices into 1-inch cubes with the crusts on. Butter inside of a 9-inch baking dish and add bread cubes. Sprinkle raisins and pecans over bread cubes. Pour milk mixture over bread cubes. Cover and refrigerate 40–60 minutes. Stir bread cubes after 30 minutes of soaking to completely submerge all bread cubes.

Preheat oven to 325°F. Bake 45–60 minutes or until pudding is firm and brown. Cool slightly and cut into squares. Serve with frozen yogurt.

Angels We Have Heard on High

Author Unknown

Angels we have heard on high,
Sweetly singing o'er the plains.
And the mountains, in reply,
Echoing their joyous strains.

Chorus:

Gloria in excelsis Deo,
Gloria in excelsis Deo.

Shepherds, why this jubilee:
Why your joyous strains prolong?
Say what may the tidings be,
Which inspire your heav'nly song!

Come to Bethlehem and see
Him whose birth the angels sing;
Come, adore on bended knee
Christ the Lord, the newborn King.

See Him in a manger laid,
Jesus, Lord of heav'n and earth!
Mary, Joseph, lend your aid,
With us sing our Savior's birth.

Chorus:

Gloria in excelsis Deo,
Gloria in excelsis Deo.

HISTORICAL NOTE:

Little is known about the origins of this beautiful carol. Scholars agree that it must have been written by someone who had a sophisticated knowledge of the Bible—perhaps a monk or priest. The Latin used in the chorus might mean that the author came from a Catholic background. And the fact that the first versions to reach publication used some French in the verse might mean that it originated there. These are clues, but they hold no definitive answer. Indeed, some scholars think "Angels We Have Heard on High" might be as old as the Christian Church itself. It may have even been written by someone who actually met Jesus.

Christ was born in the first century, yet he belongs to all centuries. He was born a Jew, yet He belongs to all races. He was born in Bethlehem, yet He belongs to all countries.

GEORGE W. TRUETT

Rules for Department Store Santas
Jenny Zink
(To employees of Western Temporary Services, world's largest supplier of Santa Clauses)

1. Santa is even-tempered.
2. Santa does not hit children over the head who kick him.
3. Santa uses the term folks rather than Mommy and Daddy because of all the broken homes.
4. Santa does not have a three-martini lunch.
5. Santa does not borrow money from store employees.
6. Santa wears a good deodorant.

Fruit Cookies

6 cups pecans

1 pound dates

3 slices pineapple

1 cup sugar

4 eggs

1 1/2 cups flour

2 tsp. baking powder

Pinch of salt

1/2 pound green or red cherries (optional)

Chop dates, pineapple, and nuts. Let set overnight with 1 tsp. vanilla. Add other ingredients. Drop by spoonfuls on greased and floured cookie sheets. Cook 15 minutes at 300°F.

Optional: Remove cookies from oven after ten minutes and place a cherry on top of each one. (If you'd like, dip the cherries in honey first.) Return cookies to oven and bake for 5 more minutes.

LOG REINDEER YARD ART

Several logs and sturdy branches
Drill and 1-inch drill bit
Red and green ribbon

Begin with a log for the body; about two feet long is a good size. Cut a short length of a slightly smaller log to act as a head. Leave the head with straight-cut ends.

Drill the body log in four places for the legs. The holes should be at least 1 1/2" deep and at a slight angle for sturdiness. Drill another hole at the top front of the body for a neck and also under the head where the neck joins.

The legs and necks are made from lengths of sturdy branches approximately 1 1/2" in diameter. Legs for deer should be long and spindly. Cut the branches for the legs to size and taper one end of each slightly with a knife. Cut another branch for the neck and taper it at both ends. Insert the tapered ends of all branches in their respective holes, add the head, and adjust the way the animal stands by sawing off the legs as necessary.

Choose two branches of a similar size to use as antlers—they should have several forks at the top for the best effect. Drill two holes at the top of the head, then insert the antlers. Add a tiny branch for a tail if desired. To dress it up, add a large bow around the neck and small bells on the antlers.

December 11

Until one feels the spirit of Christmas, there is no Christmas.
All else is outward display—so much tinsel and decorations.
For it isn't the holly, it isn't the snow. It isn't the tree,
not the firelight's glow. It's the warmth that comes to the hearts of
men when the Christmas spirit returns again.

Author Unknown

Christmas Dinner

Washington Irving

*W*hen the cloth was removed, the butler brought in a huge silver vessel of rare and curious workmanship, which he placed before the squire. Its appearance was hailed with acclamation; being the Wassail Bowl, so renowned in Christmas festivity. The contents had been prepared by the squire himself; for it was a beverage in the skilful mixture of which he particularly prided himself: alleging that it was too abstruse and complex for the comprehension of an ordinary servant. It was a potation, indeed, that might well make the heart of a toper leap within him; being composed of the richest and raciest wines, highly spiced and sweetened, with roasted apples bobbing about the surface.

The old gentleman's whole countenance beamed with a serene look of indwelling delight, as he stirred his mighty bowl. Having raised it to his lips, with a hearty wish of a merry Christmas to all present, he sent it brimming round the board, for every one to follow his example, according to the primitive style; pronouncing it "the ancient fountain of good feeling, where all hearts met together."

There was much laughing and rallying as the honest emblem of Christmas joviality circulated, and was kissed rather coyly by the ladies. ✴

CHRISTMAS BRINGS JOY TO EVERY HEART

BERNHARDT S. INGEMANN

Christmas brings joy to every heart,
Sets young and old rejoicing,
What angels sang once to all on earth,
Oh, hear the children voicing.

Bright is the tree with lights aglow,
Like birds that perch together,
The child that holdeth Christmas dear
Shall keep these joys forever.

Joy comes to all the world today,
To halls and cottage hasting,
Come, sparrow and dove, from roof tree tall,
And share our Christmas feasting.

Dance, little child, on mother's knee,
The lovely day is dawning,
The road to paradise is found
The blessèd Christmas morning.

Once to this earth our Savior came,
An infant poor and lowly,
To open for us those gardens fair
Where dwell His angels holy

Christmas joy He bringeth us,
The Christ child King of heaven,
"To every little child," He saith,
"Shall angel wings be given."

Christmas Idea: Involve your children in acts of charity by helping your family to play Santa for a needy family. Allow the children to select gifts for specific members of a preselected family, wrap them, and accompany you as you deliver them. It is even more meaningful when the children are encouraged to buy the gifts with their own money.

Christmas Idea: Encourage your children to write "Thank You" letters to Santa to be left under the tree for him when he arrives.

Christmas Idea: Involve your children in baking cookies for Santa on Christmas Eve. This offers an opportunity for them to gain a sense of giving back and keeps their young minds occupied on a day when a high state of excitement is usually the rule.

The simple shepherds heard the voice of an angel
and found their Lamb; the wise men saw the light of a star
and found their Wisdom.
FULTON JOHN SHEEN

CHRISTMAS DINNER IN PUERTO RICO

Traditional Puerto Rican Menu

Roast pork

Rice with pigeon peas

Fried plantains

Cooked green bananas

Cooked yam

Pasteles

Tembleque (coconut custard)

Arroz con dulce (rice cooked with spices, raisins, sugar, milk, and coconut milk)

The History

- Puerto Rico's Christmas season is long, starting right after Thanksgiving and officially lasting until January 6, though some draw it out even longer.
- In the days before Christmas Eve, families and friends form parrandas (similar to our carolers) and visit unsuspecting friends. They sing and play instruments (bongo, guitar, and others) and are offered food and drink as thanks.
- The parrandas stop on Christmas Eve, which is considered a solemn holiday to be spent at home with family.
- Nochebuena—Christmas dinner—takes place on Christmas Eve.
- At midnight, most families attend Christmas Mass to celebrate the birth of Jesus.
- On Christmas Day, Santa Claus brings gifts to the children.

Did You Know?

- Pasteles is a popular Nochebuena dish made of meat and vegetables wrapped in banana leaves.
- Tembleque is an authentic Puerto Rican custard dessert. The name means "quivery."
- The most popular Christmas drink is called coquito and is Puerto Rico's version of eggnog. It is prepared with coconut milk and rum.

For Our Puerto Rican Friends: Feliz Navidad, jibaros! During the holidays, Puerto Ricans love to dress up like the rural inhabitants of their country called jibaros. Many have a pava (traditional straw hat) in storage just for Christmas.

Ho! Ho! Ho!

Two little girls went to their grandmother's house for Christmas. At bedtime, the youngest one began to pray at the top of her lungs—

I want a Barbie for Christmas.
I want a Barbie for Christmas.
I want a Barbie for Christmas.

Her older sister exclaimed, "Why are you shouting? God isn't deaf!"

Her sister answered, "God's not deaf, but Grandma is!"

BISCOTTI

4 cups all-purpose flour, divided
$1/2$ tsp. baking soda
2 Tbsp. baking powder
1 stick butter, softened to room temperature
$1/2$ cup vegetable shortening
1 $1/2$ cups sugar, divided
1 tsp. vanilla extract
1 $1/2$ tsp. ground cinnamon

Combine 3 cups flour, baking soda, and baking powder; set aside. In a large bowl, cream butter, shortening, and 1 cup sugar with mixer on medium, until light and fluffy. Beat in eggs, one at a time, then vanilla until well mixed. Add flour mixture, a little at a time, until well blended. Stir in remaining flour until a soft dough forms. Add up to $1/2$ cup flour until dough is easy to handle.

Preheat oven to 350°F.

Divide dough into 4 equal pieces and form each piece of dough into an 8-inch-long log. Place 2 logs each, about 4 inches apart, on 2 ungreased cookie sheets. Use a spatula to press each log to about 2 $1/2$ inches wide. Place cookie sheets on separate oven racks. Switch cookie sheets between racks after 10 minutes of baking. Bake for a total of 20 minutes or until lightly browned and toothpick inserted in center comes out clean.

Combine cinnamon with remaining $1/2$ cup sugar. Remove cookies from oven. Transfer cookies to cutting board. Cut diagonally into $1/2$-inch-thick slices. Coat each slice with cinnamon sugar. Place slices, cut-side down, onto cookie sheets. Bake for 15 minutes. Turn slices over, and switch cookie sheets between racks. Bake for 15 minutes more or until golden. Place cookies onto wire racks to cool. Makes about 48 cookies.

HOLIDAY CHEESECAKE

Crust:
1 1/2 cups graham cracker crumbs
1/2 cup butter, melted
1/2 cup powdered sugar

Cheesecake:
3 8-ounce packages cream cheese, softened
4 eggs
1 cup sugar
1 tsp. vanilla
1 pint sour cream, room temperature
1 21-ounce can cherry or strawberry pie filling

Heat oven to 350°F. Combine graham cracker crumbs, powdered sugar, and butter. Press into bottom of an 8-inch spring-form pan. In a large bowl, beat cream cheese, eggs, sugar, and vanilla until smooth. Pour mixture over prepared crust. Bake at 350°F for 50 minutes (until center is set).

Remove from oven and spread sour cream on top of cake. Return to oven and bake an additional 5 minutes. Remove from oven and allow to cool. Spread desired topping on cheesecake. Chill overnight. Before serving, carefully remove sides from pan.

Tip: To minimize cracking, place a shallow pan half full of hot water on lower rack of oven during baking. Be sure the sour cream is room temperature when you spread it on.

Santa Claus and His Reindeer

History: The original Santa Claus, St. Nicholas, was born in Turkey in the fourth century. He was very religious from an early age, devoting his life to Christianity. He became widely known for his love of children and for his generosity. In sixteenth-century Holland, Dutch children placed their wooden shoes by the hearth in hopes that they would be filled with a treat. The Dutch spelled St. Nicholas as Sint Niklaas, which became Sinterklaas, and finally, in English, Santa Claus. In 1822, Clement C. Moore composed his famous poem, "A Visit from St. Nick," which was later published as "The Night Before Christmas."

The story of Santa's physical evolution begins in the 1600s when Santa was known by the name of Sancte Clause. It wasn't until the 1800s that the Santa Claus we know began to emerge. He was depicted as a lovable jolly fellow by the writers and artists, but the Santa Claus depicted in these pictures was of a small size. Clement Moore in the 1820s described Santa Claus as chubby and plump with a round belly that shook like a bowlful of jelly. He was dressed in a fur hat and suit, with rosy dimpled cheeks and a red cherry nose.

In 1837, the first American portrait of Santa Claus was painted by Robert Weir. Santa Claus was posed in this portrait to be wearing a stocking hat along with a short suit, starting to climb the chimney and carrying a huge bag of Christmas presents. In 1856, the elves were also added into the Santa Claus pictures. In 1863, a Santa Claus picture was painted by Thomas Nast, which showed a Santa Claus who looked like a real person. Godey's magazine's issue of December 1867 depicted an engraving of an old, bearded man, wearing a long tunic suit and carrying a staff in one hand and a doll in the other.

The final picture of Santa Claus as we know him today was given by Haddon Sundblom. His billboards and other advertisements for Coca-Cola featured a portly, grandfatherly man with human proportions and a ruddy complexion.

According to tradition, Santa's primary job is delivering presents to the children of the world on the night before Christmas. Children are encouraged to write letters to Santa listing the items they would like him to bring them. Interestingly, Santa also has a list. He records which children have been "good" and which have been "bad" during the past year. Good children receive toys and candy, and bad children receive lumps of coal.

Santa is said to live at the North Pole where he, his wife, and his elfin minions work year-round preparing gifts for the Christmas Eve deliveries. On Christmas Eve the presents are loaded and Santa takes off in a sleigh pulled by flying reindeer named Dasher, Dancer, Prancer, Vixen, Comet, Cupid, Donner, and Blitzen. Rudolph, the ninth reindeer, with a red and shiny nose, was invented in 1939 by an advertising writer for the Montgomery Ward Company.

Santa is carried by sleigh to the rooftops of homes and slides down the chimney with his bag of presents for the household. After leaving the gifts under the Christmas tree, he samples the cookies and milk left for him by excited children and magically goes up the chimney to his sleigh.

In 1925, newspapers revealed that Santa Claus in fact lives in Finnish Lapland, since grazing reindeer would not be possible at the North Pole.

Over the centuries, customs from different parts of the Northern Hemisphere came together and created international versions of Santa Claus—the timeless, deathless, white-bearded man who gives out gifts on Christmas and always returns to his home in Finnish Lapland.

December 12

Dear Lord, I've been asked, nay commanded,
to thank Thee for the Christmas turkey before us...
a turkey which was no doubt a lively, intelligent bird...
a social being...capable of actual affection...
nuzzling its young with almost human-like compassion.
Anyway, it's dead and we're gonna eat it.
Please give our respects to its family.

BERKE BREATHED

THE LUMINOUS CHRIST

ALBERT W. BEAVEN

*T*he real Christmas experience for anyone is the turning on of the light within, which comes from the spirit of the indwelling Christ. It is still his incoming that makes the difference between a darkened inn and a glorified stable.

Before we go on with our Christmas preparation, let us ask ourselves whether the real Christmas has come to us; whether what we are going through is just a form, a bartering of gifts, a forced holiday, or whether we have a real experience that makes Christmas a joy and not a bore. Christ taken in and then given out, that makes it a genuine Christmas for us and for others; for "God shined in our hearts" that the light might be passed on.

All about us are those who wait for our coming: lonely people, discouraged people, heart-sick people with little love and joy. Christmas opens our eyes and challenges us to let our light shine outside our own little circle and give cheer where it is needed most. ✶

CHRISTMAS CRESCENT COOKIES

2 sticks butter

2 cups flour

2 cups chopped pecans

5 Tbsp. sugar

2 tsp. vanilla

1 Tbsp. water

1/2 tsp. salt

Cream butter and sugar together. Add vanilla and water. Stir in flour and salt. Add pecans and mix. Divide into balls the size of walnuts. Shape the balls into crescents. Bake at 325°F for 20 minutes. While warm, roll in powdered sugar.

Say What?

Original Author Unknown

Can you identify these song titles from their descriptions?

- Oh, member of the round table with missing areas
  Oh Holy Night

- Boulder of the tinkling metal spheres
  Jingle Bell Rock

- Vehicular homicide was committed on Dad's mom by a precipitous darling
  Grandma Got Run Over By a Reindeer

- Wanted in December: top forward incisors
  All I Want For Christmas Is My Two Front Teeth

- The apartment of two psychiatrists
  The Nutcracker Suite

- The lad is a diminutive percussionist
  Little Drummer Boy

- Sir Lancelot with laryngitis
  Silent Night

- Decorate the entryways
  Deck the Halls

- Cup-shaped instruments fashioned of a whitish metallic element
  Silver Bells

- Oh small Israeli urban center
  Oh Little Town of Bethlehem

- Far off in a haybin
  Away in a Manger

- We are Kong, Lear, and Nat Cole
  We Three Kings

- Duodecimal enumeration of the passage of the yuletide season
  The Twelve Days of Christmas

- Leave and broadcast from an elevation
  Go Tell It on the Mountain

- Our fervent hope is that you thoroughly enjoy your yuletide season
  We Wish You a Merry Christmas

- Listen, the winged heavenly messengers are proclaiming tunefully
  Hark the Herald Angels Sing

- As the guardians of the woolly animals protected their charges in the dark hours
  Shepherds Watched Their Flocks by Night

- I beheld a trio of nautical vessels moving in this direction
  I Saw Three Ships

- Jubilation to the entire terrestrial globe
  Joy to the World

- Do you perceive the same vibrations which stimulate my auditory sense organ?
  Do You Hear What I Hear?

- A joyful song of reverence relative to hollow metallic vessels which vibrate and bring forth a ringing sound when struck
  Carol of the Bells

- Parent was observed osculating a red-coated unshaven teamster
  I Saw Mommy Kissing Santa Claus

- May the Deity bestow an absence of fatigue to mild male humans
  God Rest Ye Merry Gentlemen

Apple Pie

6 Jonathan or Macintosh apples, peeled, cored, and sliced

$3/4$ cup sugar

1 tsp. vanilla extract

$1/4$ tsp. ground cinnamon

1 Tbsp. all-purpose flour

2 readymade pie crusts

1 $1/2$ Tbsp. unsalted butter, cut into small pieces

Preheat oven to 450°F.

Combine apples, sugar, vanilla, cinnamon, and flour in a mixing bowl. Toss to coat apples. Place one pie crust in the bottom of a 9-inch pie pan. Gently arrange dough in pan, pressing lightly along the sides so that 1 inch hangs over edge of pan. Fill with apples and dot with butter. Cut a 3-inch slit in center of remaining pie crust and center on top of pie. Pinch overhanging dough together, roll under, and crimp with thumb and forefinger to seal dough around the edge. Place pie on a pie ring or small baking sheet to catch dripping juices.

Bake 10 minutes. Reduce temperature to 400°F. Bake 40 minutes longer or until filling is bubbly. Let cool before serving.

Simple Touches

Sometimes it is not so much what you do but how you do it that counts. You can spend a great deal of money on readymade decorations from a fancy store, or you can use a little imagination and turn your own accessories into equally appealing decorations—for free.

A dark corner that needs brightening can usually benefit from candles. Candles in all shapes, sizes, and colors can add a peaceful touch to any room. You can create a shimmering display by putting votive or tea-light candles into an assortment of unmatched goblets. To add a little extra ambiance, place the goblets on a tray, maybe in front of a mirror, and surrounded with greenery.

You can create another interesting display by stacking boxes of graduating sizes tied together with ribbon and topped with a large bow. You could also wrap plain boxes with Christmas paper and stack and tie them together in the same way. If you have a few woven baskets, find a place to group them, maybe near a fireplace. Fill them with pine cones, nuts, or clumps of Christmas greenery. For a finishing touch, tie on a bow.

For a bit of extra greenery, cut a few branches off a cedar or pine tree to lay on tabletops around other decorations. Or, you could use those branches to dress up a dining room chandelier. Simply lay the branches across the arms of the fixture. Be sure to choose greenery with stiff stems—such as pine, fir, or holly. Cut clippings about 10 to 12 inches as a rule, but size them according to your own chandelier so that they lay across two of the arms. Work your way around the fixture, adding one layer at a time until the desired fullness is reached, keeping the weight balanced so that the fixture hangs correctly. To add a colorful touch, twine bright ribbon around and through the greenery. You could also spray the greenery with artificial snow before it is arranged; add berries, small ornaments, or tiny wooden toys; add a large bow with streamers at the center; or add small bows under each light. For an added touch, insert a wooden florist's pick in the top of several apples, going through one end of a short length of ribbon. Add a bow at the top of the apple to cover the pick and tie the ribbon to the arm of the fixture.

Did You Know?

"A Visit from St. Nicholas" (also known as "'Twas the Night Before Christmas") is a poem that was first published in 1823. Many of Santa's modern attributes such as his mode of transportation, the number and names of his reindeer, and the tradition that he brings toys to children were established as a result of this publication.

Did You Know?

The "Twelve Days of Christmas" gifts included: one partridge, two turtle doves, three French hens, four calling birds, five gold rings, six geese laying, seven swans swimming, eight maids milking, nine ladies dancing, ten lords leaping, eleven pipers piping, and twelve drummers drumming. There are 364 gifts in all.

Did You Know?

It was at least two hundred years after Christ's death that Christians even thought about celebrating His birth.

Did You Know?

In 1907, Oklahoma became the last U.S. state to declare Christmas a legal holiday.

WHEN THE WISE MAN APPEARED

WILLIAM ASHLEY ANDERSON

*T*he battery in the car had gone dead; and it turned out to be a bitterly cold night, vast and empty, a ringing void domed with icy stars. Over Hallet's Hill the evening star danced like tinsel on the tip of a Christmas tree. The still air was resonant as the inside of an iron bell; but within our snug farmhouse it was mellow with the warmth of three cherry-red stoves. The dinner things had been pushed back, and I was feeling relaxed and content, lazily smoking a cigarette, when Bruce came into the room.

He had gone upstairs in heavy boots and flannel cruiser's shirt. He reappeared in a long white nightgown with a purple cloak of Tintexed cotton over his shoulders. In one hand he held a tall crown of yellow pasteboard and tinsel. From the other swung an ornate censer. His boots had been replaced by thin flapping sandals.

"What in the world are you supposed to be?" I asked.

My wife looked at him critically. There was both concern and tenderness in the look. Women always look tenderly at Bruce; and then, of course, she had more than a hand in his costuming. She said indignantly:

"He's one of the Wise Men of the East!"

Virginia, my daughter, put both hands to her face, ready to stifle an hysterical shriek because Bruce, who is small for fourteen, likes to be grouped with men, swinging a double-edged axe with the best of them and handling a twelve-gauge as if it were a BB gun. With a tight voice she managed to say:

"Have you got matches for that thing?"

With considerable difficulty Bruce raised his skirts and produced a box from his pants pocket.

"He'll be ready," said my wife, "whatever happens!" She looked at me, and I thought again how lovely she is. That did me no good. Her look was an urgent reminder. I felt all the chill of the night air run up my spine, suddenly remembering that I had promised to get the boy to the school-house in town in good time for the Christmas pageant. I shuddered and groaned and went out into the night pulling on a heavy coat.

By one of those freaks of mechanical whimsy that baffle man, its maker, the engine caught at the first turn of the crank, and off we went with a bang, bouncing and roaring across the rough frozen field. That was a trick of the devil.

At the turn by the barn the generator couldn't pick up enough current; and there the engine died. My heart sank with its last long sigh. I looked out the side of my eyes at Bruce, sitting there saying nothing, making me think what a kid he still is, with the crown and censer clasped in his arms, staring down that long endless lane that disappeared in the lonely hills.

It was a moment of deep breathless silence. The hills walled us in from all hope of neighborly assistance. Hallet's place was more than a mile and a half away, and the nearest turn of Route 90, even with the thin chance of a lift, was more than two miles away. Still, what could I do about it? I felt as helpless as a kid myself—and I had promised to get him there on time.

Well, I thought, it's not tragically important. Bruce said nothing, but his eyes were wide, staring now at the big star twinkling just over the ragged edge of the mountain. Then a strange and uneasy feeling stirred in me, because I knew the boy was praying. He had made his promises too!

Before I could move, he dropped his crown and censer and scrambled out of the car, stumbling over his skirts. But all his straining and heaving at the crank was useless. I strained and heaved in turn and was equally impotent. When we weren't sweating we were shivering. The still air cut like knives. The cold metal clung to our hands. Every deep breath rasped my lungs until I sputtered.

Ordinarily we might have pushed the car to the edge of the rise and rolled it down the hill in gear; but the grease stuck like cement, and we couldn't budge it. After a while I straightened my cramped back and guessed I'd smoke a cigarette while I thought it over. When I struck a light with fumbling hands and looked up through the smoke Bruce was scuttling down the lane, one hand holding his skirts, one hand swinging the censer, the high golden crown perched cock-eyed on his head. I hesitated between laughing at him and yelling for him to stop. At the moment it seemed that this was about the only thing he could do. As for me, there wasn't anything I could do. Then I thought of the expression on his face as he prayed, and I felt mean, realizing that a man's view and a boy's view are not necessarily the same.

I threw the cigarette away and began once more to crank.

I don't know how long the struggle lasted, but all at once the engine sneezed. With hands clenched and eyes closed I straightened slowly and held my breath. The engine began to cough throatily. I scrambled frenziedly into the car.

Just about where Fifth Street enters Stroudsburg I overtook Bruce. There was a twist at my innards at the sight of that small figure trudging along with the cock-eyed crown on his head and the censer hugged to his stomach. A long sigh went out of me as he turned his face into the lights with a white-lipped grin. His gown was torn and he shivered violently.

"You shouldn't have gone off that way," I growled. "It's too cold. It's terribly cold!"

"I put twigs in the censer," he said, "and made a fire. I kept warm enough."

"But look at your feet! You might have frozen them!"

"It wasn't so bad. I took a bearing on the star and made a short cut across Lasoine's farm. It came out right back there by the new cottage."

After that I was too busy putting on speed to say much. We arrived at the school on time. I stood in back and watched.

A good many years had passed since I last saw the story of Bethlehem and the homage of the Three Wise Men presented by children at Christmastime. It had become so old a story to me that it seemed strange to realize that to them it was new.

When I saw Bruce walking stiff-legged on cut and chilblained feet with his two companions on the stage, kneeling by the crèche, declaiming his studied lines, first I regretted my laughter at the dinner table, then an uneasy awe rose up within me.

Going home we stopped at a garage for anti-freeze and at a soda-counter for hot chocolate, and I said nothing but commonplace things. As we rolled comfortably out of Fifth Street Bruce showed me where the short-cut came out.

"That's where the Thompsons lived," I said, "before the place burned down."

"I know," said Bruce, "where the boy was burned to death."

A new house had been built on the old foundations, and people were again living there.

"They've got lights burning."

As we passed the Lasoine farm there were lights burning there too. I thought this was strange, because since George Lasoine had gone off to war the old grandmother, who had lost her youngest son in the first war, had sort of shriveled up, and a gloom lay over the house; but as I slowed down I could see Lou Lasoine through the kitchen window, smoking his pipe and smiling at the two women talking, so I sensed everything was all right.

So far as I knew that was about all there was to the evening; but on Christmas Day the Good Farmer's Wife came by with gifts of mincemeat made from venison and a jug of sassafras cider. She had shaken off her customary pessimism and was full of bounce and high-pitched talk. I heard the laughter and ejaculations in the kitchen where my wife was supervising the Christmas feast; and since I have a weakness for the racy gossip of the countryside, I drifted toward the kitchen too.

"You must hear this!" said my wife, drawing me in.

The Farmer's Wife looked at me with a glittering wary eye.

"You hain't agoin' to believe it either," she said. "Just the same I'm tellin' you, folks up here in the hills see things and they do believe."

"What have you been seeing?"

"It was old Mrs. Lasoine. Last Tuesday night when she was a-feelin' awful low she thought she heard something back of the barn and she looked out. Now I'll say this for the old lady—she's got good vision. That she has! Plenty good! There warn't no moonlight, but if you recollect it was a bright starry night. And there she saw, plain as her own husband, one of the Wise Men of the Bible come a-walkin' along the hill with a gold crown on his head, a-swingin' one of them pots with smoke in them—"

My mouth opened, and I looked at Rosamunde, and Rosamunde looked at me; but before I could say anything, the Farmer's Wife hurried on:

"Now don't you start a-laughin'—not yet!—'cause that hain't the long and short of it! There's other testimony! The Thompsons. You know the ones whose oldest boy was burned in the fire? Well, there it was the children. First, they heard him, they heard him a-singin' 'Come All Ye Faithful' plain as day. They went runnin' to the window and they seen the Wise Man a-walkin' in the starlight across the lane, gold crown and robes and firepot and all! Well, my goodness, they put up such a-shoutin' and a-yellin' that their parents come a-runnin'. But by then it was too late. He was gone. Just disappeared. Afterward they went out and looked but couldn't find hide nor hair—"

"Did they see any other signs?" I asked faintly.

The Farmer's Wife scoffed.

"Old folks and children see things which maybe we can't. All I can say is this. Lasoines and Thompsons don't even know each other. But old lady

Lasoine was heartsick and lonely and a-prayin' about her lost boy, and the Thompsons was heartsick and lonely because this was the first Christmas in the new house without Harry, and you dassent say they wasn't a-prayin' too! Maybe you don't believe that amounts to anythin'—but I'm tellin' you it was a comfort to them to see and believe!"

I swallowed hard, recalling the look on Bruce's face as he stared at the star, when I knew he was praying that he might not fail his friends. Well, not daring to look at my wife, I said with all the sincerity I could feel:

"Yes, I believe God was close that night."

For the first time in her garrulous life the Farmer's Wife was stricken dumb. She looked at me as if an even greater miracle had been performed before her very eyes. ✳

WILLIAM ASHLEY ANDERSON (1890–1988)
Advertising executive and short-story writer, Anderson was born in Red Bank, New Jersey. His humor and careful attention to dialect paint a vivid picture for his readers.

Let us remember that the Christmas heart is a
giving heart, a wide open heart that thinks of others first.
The birth of the baby Jesus stands as the most significant event in
all history, because it has meant the pouring into a sick world of the
healing medicine of love which has transformed all manner of hearts
for almost two thousand years.... Underneath all the bulging
bundles is this beating Christmas heart.

GEORGE MATTHEW ADAMS

December 13

She will have a son, and you are to name him Jesus, for he will save his people from their sins. All of this occurred to fulfill the Lord's message through his prophet:

> "Look! The virgin will conceive a child!
> She will give birth to a son,
> and they will call him Immanuel,
> which means, 'God is with us.'"
> (Matthew 1:21–23, NLT)

A Gift for Each of Us

FIRST BAPTIST CHURCH BULLETIN

SYRACUSE, NEW YORK

There was a gift for each of us left under the tree of life 2000 years ago by Him whose birthday we celebrate today. The gift was withheld from no man. Some have left the packages unclaimed. Some have accepted the gift and carry it around, but have failed to remove the wrapping and look inside to discover the hidden splendor. The packages are all alike: in each is a scroll on which is written, "All that the Father hath is thine." Take and live!✲

Did You Know?

America's official national Christmas tree is located in Kings Canyon National Park in California. The tree, a giant sequoia called the "General Grant Tree," is over 90 meters (300 feet) high. It was made the official Christmas tree in 1925.

Gift Idea for Grandparents

Decorate T-shirts for Grandma and Grandpa with their grandchild's handprints or footprints on the front. Let your child choose the gift-wrap and help you wrap the package. This is a grandparent's dream!

All My Heart
This Night Rejoices

Paul Gerhardt

All my heart this night rejoices,

As I hear,

Far and near,

Sweetest angel voices:

"Christ is born" their choirs are singing.

Till the air,

Everywhere,

Now with joy is ringing.

Hark! A voice from yonder manger,

Soft and sweet,

Doth entreat,

"Flee from woe and danger;

Brethren come; from all that grieves you

You are freed;

All you need

I will surely give you."

Come, then, let us hasten yonder;

Here let all,

Great and small,

Love Him who with love is yearning;

Hail the Star

That from far

Bright with hope is burning.

Thee, dear Lord, with heed I'll cherish,

Live to Thee,

And with Thee

Dying, shall not perish,

But shall dwell with Thee forever

Far on high

In the joy

That can alter never.

CHRISTMAS DINNER IN ARGENTINA

Traditional Argentinian Menu

Suckling pig

Ninos envuettas (steak rolls)

Roast pork

Stuffed tomatoes

Mince pies

Sweet breads

Pudding

The History

- Argentina comprises almost all of the southern part of Latin America, bordering the South Atlantic Ocean, between Chile and Uruguay. Argentina is a country with many enriching cultural influences, so its Christmas customs are varied and very difficult to generalize.
- Unlike the U.S., Christmas in Argentina is celebrated in the summer.
- Despite the warm weather, Christmas trees are part of the celebration,

usually ornamented with colored lights, knickknacks, and candles. Many families add cotton to the tree to replicate snow.

- Argentines typically attend church before coming together for dinner.
- To take advantage of the warm weather, Christmas dinner often takes the form of a picnic or barbeque, followed by champagne and a variety of delicious cakes.

Did You Know?

- Ninos envuettas is steak cut in pieces three inches square, stuffed with minced meat mixed with onions, hard-boiled eggs, and spices. The meat is shaped in rolls, browned, and baked or simmered until tender.
- The eagerly awaited Christmas toast is a drink prepared with different kinds of fruit cut into pieces and mixed with juice and cider.
- Fireworks are common around midnight.

For Our Argentinian Friends: December 24 is a very long day. Family and friends prepare a Christmas feast, which is eaten late in the evening. Afterward, everyone waits patiently for the stroke of midnight to open their gifts.

My idea of Christmas, whether old-fashioned or modern, is very simple: loving others. Come to think of it, why do we have to wait for Christmas to do that?

Bob Hope

PUMPKIN PIE

2 cups milk, scalded

2 cups pumpkin, cooked and strained

1 cup maple syrup

$1/8$ cup sugar

1 Tbsp. flour

$1/2$ tsp. salt

1 tsp. ginger

1 tsp. cinnamon

$1/4$ tsp. nutmeg (optional)

2 large eggs, beaten

1 unbaked 9-inch pie shell

Blend first ten ingredients together. Pour into the unbaked pie shell. Bake at 350°F for 45 minutes or until set. Let cool and serve.

Tip: Prepare the raw pumpkin by scraping out the inside, skinning and cutting into 1-inch cubes. Bake at 350°F for an hour and then turn off the heat. Leave the pumpkin in the oven for another hour or two to reduce the moisture content. A 10-inch diameter pumpkin will make 4 to 6 pies.

Tip: This recipe replaces much of the sugar normally found in a pumpkin pie recipe with maple syrup. Use only real 100 percent maple syrup, not maple flavored pancake syrup, as their sugar content is different. You can use brown sugar instead of maple syrup.

Tip: You can test whether the pie is done by inserting a clean table knife into the center. If the knife comes out clean, the pie is done.

CHRISTMAS STOCKINGS

History: According to a very old tradition, the original Saint Nicholas left his first gifts of gold coins in the stockings of three poor girls who needed the money for their wedding dowries. The story goes like this:

Once upon a time, there was a kind nobleman whose wife died of an illness, leaving him with three daughters to raise. The poor man suffered another blow when he lost all his money in failed business endeavors. The family was impoverished and forced to move into a peasant's cottage, where the daughters were responsible for the cooking, sewing, and cleaning.

When it came time for the girls to marry, the nobleman became even more depressed. Having no money or property, he could provide nothing for his daughters' dowries.

One Christmas Eve night, the nobleman's daughters washed out their clothing and hung their stockings over the fireplace to dry. That night Saint Nicholas, knowing the despair of the father, stopped by the house. Looking in the window, he saw that the family had gone to bed. He also noticed the daughters' stockings hanging on the hearth. Struck by an inspiration, Saint Nicholas took three small bags of gold from his pouch and threw them one by one down the chimney. Nicholas, being quite a remarkable fellow, was able to get the bags cleanly into the stockings.

The next morning when the young women awoke, they retrieved their stockings and found the bags of gold—enough for ample dowries. The aging nobleman was able to see his three daughters safely married.

The tradition of hanging stockings by the fireplace continues to this day. Until recent times, youngsters could expect to receive small items like fruit, nuts, and candy. Several decades ago, it became customary to include "stocking stuffers," small inexpensive gifts. In recent times, even expensive gifts often grace the well-hung stocking.

Although originally people hung real stockings, that rarely happens anymore. Christmas stockings can be store-bought or homemade. They typically amount to cloth sacks cut in the shape of stockings. They can be made of almost any fabric from satin to burlap to quilted patches. They are often hand decorated and have the name of the person emblazoned at the top.

This tradition is observed in other countries as well. In France, the children place their shoes by the fireplace. In Holland, the children fill their shoes with hay and a carrot for the horse of Sinterklaas. In Hungary, children shine their shoes before putting them near the door or a windowsill. Italian children leave their shoes out the night before Epiphany on January 5. And in Puerto Rico, children put greens and flowers in small boxes and place them under their beds for the camels of the Three Kings. The idea to put a lump of coal in the stockings of misbehaving children originated in Italy.

Christmas Idea: Bring the family together at bedtime on Christmas Eve and make the hanging of the Christmas stockings the last activity of the evening. Place hooks on the mantel, stairs, or the doorway so the stockings can be easily and safely hung. When all the stockings are in their places, hold hands in a circle for a Christmas-night prayer. Then carry the children directly to their beds.

Christmas Idea: Make the hanging of the Christmas stockings part of a larger late-evening tradition that includes the reading of the

Christmas story from the book of Luke and family prayer. Serve hot chocolate—a perfect drink to rest and relax the brain for sleep. End the evening by having the children hang their stockings.

Christmas Idea: Allow your children to decorate their own Christmas stockings with items of significance from the past year. These can be glued to the fabric or pinned for easy removal. After the children have gone to bed, take pictures of the stockings for your album. This also serves as a reminder of how your children chose to decorate their stockings through the years.

Nothing Says Love Like a Letter

The simple act of letter writing can be a wonderful Christmas gift, especially for an older person. Begin with a personal greeting and some thoughts about how you know the person or special memories from your relationship. Make your letter personal, including interesting events from your everyday life—our dog had puppies or a description of this year's Christmas program, for example. Don't brag; keep it real. Close with a show of genuine concern.

A special letter can also make a wonderful keepsake gift for a child or grandchild. Write about your memories—the day they were born, the day they started school, the day they graduated from college, the day they got married, a special vacation together, time spent at your home—the options are endless.

Package your letters in decorated envelopes. Mail or hang on the tree.

Holiday Bows

Clothespin

Spray paint any color: red, green, gold, etc.

48" (7/8" wide) nonwoven-edge ribbon

Thin floral wire

Small pine cones, acorns

Dried plants or flowers such as statice or lycopodium

Spray the clothespin with paint. Make a bow by looping the ribbon and holding it with a short piece of floral wire twisted around the center. Fluff out the loops of the bow before attaching to the top of the clothespin with hot glue. Glue a trimming of natural cones or acorns surrounded by statice and lycopodium onto the center of the bow.

Clip clothespin bow onto everything from drapes and dinner napkins to the tree.

What Child Is This?

William Chatterton Dix

What child is this, who, laid to rest,
On Mary's lap is sleeping?
Whom Angels greet with anthems sweet,
While shepherds watch are keeping?
This, this is Christ the King,
Whom shepherds guard and angels sing:
Haste, haste to bring him laud,
The babe, the son of Mary.

Why lies he in such mean estate
Where ox and ass are feeding?
Good Christian, fear: for sinners here
The silent Word is pleading.
Nails, spear shall pierce Him through,
The cross be borne for me, for you.
Hail, Hail, the Word made flesh,
The babe, the son of Mary.

So bring him incense, gold, and myrrh.
Come, peasant, king, to own him,
The King of kings salvation brings,
Let loving hearts enthrone him.
Raise, raise a song on high,
The virgin sings her lullaby.
Joy, Joy for Christ is born
The babe, the son of Mary.

About the time of the Civil War, a young family man spent his days working hard to support his family. It was in his spare time that William Chatterton Dix pursued his passion—poetry. For years he wrote on a variety of topics without much success. That changed the day he sat down and, in one sitting, penned the words to a beautiful poem he titled "The Manger Throne."

The popularity of Dix's poem continued to grow until it was finally coupled with music—the hauntingly beautiful folk melody known as "Greensleeves." Easy to sing and lovely to listen to, the poem—now a Christmas carol known as "What Child Is This?"—became greatly loved.

Someone is shouting:
"Clear a path in the desert!
Make a straight road
for the Lord our God.
Fill in the valleys;
flatten every hill
and mountain.
Level the rough
and rugged ground.
Then the glory of the Lord
will appear for all to see.
The Lord has promised this!"
(Isaiah 40:3–5, cev)

December 14

CHRISTMAS JOY

JOHN GREENLEAF WHITTIER

Somehow, not only for Christmas
But all the long year through,
The joy you give to others
Is the joy that comes back to you.
And the more you spend in blessing
The poor and lonely and sad,
The more of your heart's possessing
Returns to you glad.

Paper Sack Christmas

Elece Hollis

he lines spoken weren't clear, but of course we all knew the story. The plot wasn't hard to follow. The sound system buzzed and crackled. Children giggled and poked each other with freckled elbows. Soon the wise men in bath robes and cardboard crowns made their grand entry and Joseph hustled Mary and Jesus off to safety in Egypt. An older man, the pastor, I presumed, flipped on the lights and declared the play "Our best ever!" He called for the band of crumple-winged angels, who came skipping up to help him pass out the Christmas bags.

Oh my goodness—Christmas bags! I thought as my mind raced back to a story my mother had told me as a child.

Her family was poor. Little wonder—everyone was poor in Oklahoma in 1933, but most were not accustomed to poverty. It had crept up behind them and jumped on them like a hungry, snarling cat on an unsuspecting prey, tearing apart families, homes and dreams. My mother's family made out better than most because my grandfather, Papa, owned a small neighborhood grocery store. In the now non-existent town of Tribbey, Oklahoma, Papa's store served as gas station, post office, grocery, and general meeting place.

At his wooden counter, a roller of brown wrapping paper and a string dispenser resided beside an ornate cash register and a porcelain grocer's scale. The register had long since grown silent. The cash drawer sat open, no cash went in or out—no change changed hands. To be sure, Papa couldn't stock the store as well as he'd been able to before the crash. But, people still had to eat, and they had need of sewing needles and spools of thread, besides the basics like flour, sugar, beans, kerosene, and coffee. Normally, folks grew their own garden vegetables, but the drought had put an end to that. Even raising chickens and hunting and fishing became non-productive as the dust bowl settled down over the state, smothering hope.

Papa gave credit and vowed he would continue as long as he could get anything to sell, and as long as he could feed his own family. There were canned goods gathering dust on the shelves behind the counter. Dill pickles languished in brine barrels. Peppermints, lemon drops, and horehound candies slowly crystallized in bell jars. Bolts of cloth mellowed on the exposed rolled edges that faced out into the store. Light from the two front windows and four bare bulbs hanging suspended from white ceramic fixtures had faded them.

The depression had faded Papa too. It aged him. It hurt him to see children hungry and ragged. It pained him to watch friends and neighbors lose their farms and be forced onto the roads. So Papa gave credit in a time when it made no sense to give credit, when chances of recouping his losses were surely non-existent.

Papa trusted people, and very few took his trust lightly. Some, of course, were never able to repay his goodness. They left in old ramshackle automobiles westward into the heat and wind, gray with dust, to California. They lived like gypsies in tents and old trucks picking fruit at negligible wages. In the years after the depression, checks came like writer's royalty checks, belated and unexpected in the mail with notes that said things like, "You gave us credit for food stuffs through our hardest year. Thank you. Here is a check for the bill of $43.51 that we owed you." They were payments on accounts that Papa had long since deleted from his books, debts forgiven.

It grieved Papa that many folks would not accept help no matter how terribly their children needed things. He liked to give penny candy to the children who came into his store. He especially hurt for those wearing hungry faces that seemed to cry out for something sweet. Those children would

shake their heads and say staunchly, "We don't take charity, Mr. Michael."
Finally, one Christmas as Papa contemplated the pain of watching children
pass the holidays without a visit from Santa Claus or even a peppermint
stick in their stockings, he came up with a plan. If every child in town were
presented with a treat, then no one could define the treats as "charity."

So Papa went to work. He rounded up the languishing bags of candy no
one could afford to buy, and ordered in extra fruit and a big bag of nuts.
Then the whole family helped fill the brown paper lunch bags. On the night
of the school Christmas program, Santa (Grandma, dressed in a red suit
and a huge black belt and sporting a cotton beard) bustled to the front of
the overcrowded classroom and passed a bag to every person present. Papa
was thrilled. He had gotten in a lick on those bullies—poverty and pride. He
had spread some happiness in the midst of the harsh times. If possible he
enjoyed it more than the hungriest kid there!

Now in many rural Oklahoma towns the tradition of the paper sacks
at Christmas is still alive and well. Visiting the small church to watch the
"Our best ever!" play a few years ago, I was delighted when a grinning
angel passed me a small brown bag of fruit, nuts, and candies. In such
prosperous times when children eat sweets daily and an orange is not even
considered a treat, the tradition lingered. To the children it was a novelty.
To the survivors the sacks were proof of the fact that the depression had
not whipped them.[6] ✶

Did You Know?

After *A Christmas Carol*, Charles Dickens wrote several other Christmas
stories, one each year, but none was as successful as the original.

CHRISTMAS DINNER IN GREECE

Traditional Greek Menu

Turkey stuffed with meat, tomatoes, and red currants

Roast lamb or pork

Fricassees (lamb or pork cooked with egg and lemon sauce)

Christopsomo (Christmas bread)

Melomakarona (sweet honey-covered biscuits)

Kourabiedes (icing- or sugar-coated biscuits)

The History

- In some regions an olive branch is stuck into the Christmas cake and placed in the center of the table in place of a Christmas tree.

- Tradition requires that the table be lifted up three times while all recite "Table of Our Lady, Table of the Virgin Mary, Christ is born, let all the world rejoice." The cake and branch stay in the center of the table until Epiphany, when the cake is cut.

- The Kalanda, or Christmas carols, are traditionally sung on Christmas Eve, New Year's Eve, and the Eve of Epiphany. Groups of children go from house to house singing the appropriate carol for the day—there is a special song for each of the three holidays—usually accompanied by metal triangles (trigono). They will ask the house owner "na ta poume?" (literally "shall we sing it?") before beginning, in order to ensure that the family is not mourning the recent death of a family member. Afterward, the children are given sweets or coins by the house owner.

- The custom of the turkey for Christmas arrived in Europe from Mexico in 1824. It is now widely used in Greece and has almost replaced the pork meat for holiday fare—but not completely.

Did You Know?

- In olden times it was the custom for each family in the village to raise a pig or hog (*hiros* in Greek), which would be slaughtered on Christmas Eve and served as the main holiday dish the next day.
- The mother marks the Christmas bread with her handprint before baking it, a sign to the children that Jesus, too, has touched the bread on this holy day.

For Our Greek Friends: Take heart! It will soon be time to open those gifts! In Greek tradition, St. Basil's (Agios Vassilis) name has been given to Father Christmas. St. Vassilis Day is celebrated on January 1; therefore the Greek Agios Vassilis—Father Christmas—leaves presents for the children on New Year's Day rather than Christmas Day.

Family Christmas Gift Idea

Put together a cookbook containing favorite family recipes and make copies for moms and dads, sisters and brothers, aunts and uncles, even grandparents. If you are having a Christmas party for the whole gang, pass them around and let family members autograph their recipes. What a special family keepsake!

Christmas is the season of joy,
of holiday greetings exchanged,
of gift-giving, and of families united.

NORMAN VINCENT PEALE

Go Tell It on the Mountain

Frederick Jerome Work

While shepherds kept their watching o'er silent flocks by night,
Behold throughout the heavens there shone a holy light.
Go, tell it on the mountain over the hills and everywhere
Go, tell it on the mountain that Jesus Christ is born.

The shepherds feared and trembled when lo! above the earth
Rang out the angel chorus that hailed our Savior's birth;
Go, tell it on the mountain over the hills and everywhere
Go, tell it on the mountain that Jesus Christ is born.

Down in a lowly manger our humble Christ was born;
And God sent us salvation that blessed Christmas morn.
Go, tell it on the mountain over the hills and everywhere
Go, tell it on the mountain that Jesus Christ is born.

When I was a seeker I sought both night and day
I sought the Lord to help me and He showed me the way.
Go, tell it on the mountain over the hills and everywhere
Go, tell it on the mountain that Jesus Christ is born.

He made me a watchman upon the city wall
And if I am a Christian I am the least of all.
Go, tell it on the mountain over the hills and everywhere
Go, tell it on the mountain that Jesus Christ is born.

HISTORICAL NOTE:

Historians disagree about the origins of this Christmas song. Some attribute it to an anonymous writer while others believe it was the work of a black composer, teacher, and scholar named Frederick Jerome Work who specialized in the collection, arrangement, and distribution of black spirituals. First published in the early 1900s, the song did not become popular until the 1950s.

GILDED WALNUTS

English walnuts

2-inch strips of white paper

Stylus or fountain pen

Plastic pushpins

Glue

Shellac

Gold-leaf paint

3-inch strips of green and red ribbon

Write a blessing or affirmation on the paper strips—one for each walnut. Break open the walnuts and remove the meat from the shell. Clean it out well. Fold the paper and place it inside the shell. Glue the halves of the shell back together.

When dry, work the plastic pushpin into the end of the walnut. Paint the shell, including the tack. When dry, paint with shellac. Tie a ribbon to the pin and hang it from the tree. At your Christmas gathering, allow friends and family members to take a walnut, crack it open, and read the blessing inside.

Figgy Pudding

1/2 pound dried figs

1/4 cup fluffy breadcrumbs

1 cup almonds or walnuts, chopped

1 cup light brown sugar

3/4 cup candied citrus peel

3 Tbsp. melted butter

4 eggs, beaten

1/2 tsp. cinnamon

1/4 tsp. nutmeg

Chop the figs and mix with crumbs. Brown the almonds or walnuts. Mix with other ingredients. Put the mixture into a greased mold and bake at 325°F for 1 hour.

Hard Sauce:

Beat 1 cup of butter for about 2 minutes. Add a cup of icing sugar and 1 Tbsp. vanilla. Beat for 5 minutes. Pour over hot pudding.

THE STAR

FLORENCE M. KINGSLEY

*O*nce upon a time in a country far away, there lived a little girl named Ruth. Ruth's home was not at all like our houses, for she lived in a little tower on top of the great stone wall that surrounded the town of Bethlehem.

Ruth's father was the hotelkeeper—the Bible says the "innkeeper." This inn was not at all like our hotels of today. There was a great open yard, which was called the courtyard. All about this yard were little rooms, and each traveler who came to the hotel rented one.

This inn stood near the great stone wall of the city, so that as Ruth stood one night, looking out of the tower window, she looked directly into the courtyard. It was truly a strange sight that met her eyes. So many people were coming to the inn, for the king had made a law that every man should return to the city where his father used to live to be counted and to pay taxes.

Some of the people came on the backs of camels, with great rolls of bedding and their dishes for cooking upon the back of the beast. Some came on little donkeys, and on their backs, too, were the bedding and the dishes. Some people came walking—slowly, for they were very tired.

As Ruth looked down into the courtyard, she saw camels being led to their places by their masters; she heard the snap of the whips; she saw the sparks shoot up from the fires that were kindled in the courtyard where each person was preparing for his own supper; she heard the cries of the tired, hungry, little children.

Presently her mother, who was cooking supper, came over to the window and said, "Ruthie, thou shalt hide in the house until all those people are gone. Dost thou understand?"

"Yes, my mother," said the child, and she left the window to follow her mother back to the stove, limping painfully, for little Ruth was a cripple. Her mother stooped suddenly and caught the child in her arms.

"My poor little lamb. It was a mule's kick, just six years ago, that hurt your poor back and made you lame."

"Never mind, my mother. My back does not ache today, and lately, when the light of the strange new star has shone down upon my bed, my back has felt so much stronger, and I have felt so happy, as though I could climb above the stars!"

Her mother shook her head sadly. "Thou art not likely to climb much, now or ever, but come, the supper is ready; let us go and find your father. I wonder what keeps him?"

They found the father standing at the gate of the courtyard, talking to a man and woman who had just arrived. The man was tall, with a long beard, and he led by a rope a snow-white mule, on which sat the drooping figure of the woman. As Ruth and her mother came near, they heard the father say, "But I tell thee that there is no more room in the inn. Hast thou no friends where thou canst go to spend the night?" The man shook his head. "No, none," he answered. "I care not for myself, but my poor wife." Little Ruth pulled at her mother's dress. "Mother, the oxen sleep out under the stars these warm nights, and the straw is clean and warm; I have made a bed there for my little lamb."

Ruth's mother bowed before the tall man. "Thou didst hear the child. It is as she says—the straw is clean and warm." The tall man bowed his head. "We shall be very glad to stay," and he helped the sweet-faced woman down from the mule's back and led her away to the cave-stable, while little Ruth and her mother hurried up the stairs that they might send a bowl of porridge to the sweet-faced woman and a cup of milk, as well.

That night when little Ruth lay down on her bed, the rays of the beautiful new star shone through the window more brightly than before. They seemed to soothe her tired, aching shoulders. She fell asleep and dreamed that the beautiful, bright star burst, and out of it came countless angels, who sang in the night: "Glory to God in the highest, peace on earth, good-will toward men."

And then it was morning and her mother was bending over her, saying, "Awake, awake, little Ruth. Mother has something to tell thee." Then as her eyes opened slowly her mother said, "Angels came in the night, little one, and left a Baby to lay beside your little white lamb in the manger."

That afternoon Ruth went with her mother to the fountain. The mother turned to talk to the other women of the town about the strange things heard and seen the night before, but Ruth went on and sat down by the edge of the fountain. The child was not frightened, for strangers came often to the well; but never before had she seen men who looked like the three who now came toward her. The first one, a tall man with a long, white beard, came close to Ruth and said, "Canst thou tell us, child, where is born He that is called King of the Jews?"

"I know of no king," answered Ruth, "but last night while the star was shining, the angels brought a baby to lie beside my little white lamb in the manger." The stranger bowed his head. "That must be He. Wilt thou show me the way to Him, my child?" So Ruth ran and her mother led the three men to the cave, "and when they saw the Child, they rejoiced with exceeding great joy, and opening their gifts, they presented unto Him gold and frankincense and myrrh," with wonderful jewels, so that Ruth's mother's eyes opened with wonder, but little Ruth saw only the Baby, who lay asleep on His mother's breast.

If I might only hold Him in my arms, thought she, but she was afraid to ask.

After a few days, the strangers left Bethlehem, all but the three—the man, whose name was Joseph, and Mary his wife, and the Baby. Then, as of old, little Ruth played about the courtyard, and the white lamb frolicked at her side. Often she dropped to her knees to press the little woolly white head against her breast, while she murmured: "My little lamb, my very, very own. I love you, lambie," and then together they would steal over to the entrance of the cave to peep in at the Baby, and always Ruth thought, *If I might only touch His hand.* But she was afraid to ask.

One night as she lay in her bed she thought to herself: *Oh, I wish I had a beautiful gift for Him, such as the wise men brought; but I have nothing at all to offer, and I love Him so much.* Just then the light of the star, which was nightly fading, fell across the foot of the bed and shone full upon the white lamb which lay asleep at her feet—and then she thought of something.

The next morning she arose with her face shining with joy. She dressed carefully and with the white lamb held close to her breast, went slowly and painfully down the stairway and over to the door of the cave. "I have come," she said, "to worship Him, and I have brought Him—my little, white lamb." The mother smiled at the lame child, then she lifted the Baby from her breast and placed Him in the arms of the little maid who knelt at her feet.

A few days later an angel came to the father, Joseph, and told him to take the Baby and hurry into the land of Egypt, for the wicked king wanted to do Him harm; and so these three—the father, the mother, and the Baby—went by night to that far country of Egypt. And the star grew dimmer and dimmer and passed away forever from the skies of Bethlehem; but little Ruth grew straight and strong and beautiful as the almond trees in the orchard, and all the people who saw her were amazed, for Ruth was once a cripple.

"It was the light of the strange star," her mother said; but little Ruth knew it was the touch of the blessed Christ Child, who was once folded against her heart. ✳

FLORENCE M. KINGSLEY (1859–1937)

The writer of this wonderful story was better known for three powerful books set during biblical times. In 1894, a publisher commissioned a writing contest. The instruction that the stories should "set a child's heart on fire for Christ" caught her attention, and she sent in a story about Titus. For her effort, she was awarded $1,000. Eventually the book sold more than two hundred thousand copies and Kingsley wrote a sequel. Kingsley's knowledge of biblical history and her literary skill were a rare and compelling combination.

God grant you the light of Christmas, which is faith;
the warmth of Christmas, which is love;
the radiance of Christmas, which is purity;
the righteousness of Christmas, which is justice;
the belief in Christmas, which is truth;
and all of Christmas, which is Christ.

WILDA ENGLISH

December 15

Christmas, my child, is love in action...
When you love someone, you give to them as God gives to us.
The greatest gift He ever gave was the Person of His Son,
sent to us in human form so that we might know what
God the Father is really like! Every time we love,
every time we give, it's Christmas.

DALE EVANS ROGERS

CHRISTMAS IN THE MANSION

AUTHOR UNKNOWN

It is Christmas in the mansion,
Yule-log fires and silken frocks;
It is Christmas in the cottage,
Mother's filling little socks.

It is Christmas on the highway,
In the thronging, busy mart;
But the dearest, truest Christmas
Is the Christmas in the heart.

So remember while December
Brings the only Christmas Day,
In the year let there be Christmas
In the things you do and say.

Wouldn't life be worth the living
Wouldn't dreams be coming true
If we kept the Christmas spirit
All the whole year through.

Victorian Christmas Card Greeting

Author Unknown

Oh, life is but a river;
And in our childhood, we
But a fair running streamlet
Adorn'd with flowers see.

But as we grow more earnest,
The river grows more deep;
And where we laugh'd in childhood
We, older, pause to weep

Each Christmas as it passes,
some change to us doth bring;
Yet to our friends the closer,
As time creeps on, we cling.

*It is good to be children sometimes,
and never better than at Christmas,
when its mighty Founder was a child Himself.*

Charles Dickens

CHRISTMAS FUDGE

3 cups (18 ounces) semisweet chocolate chips
1 can sweetened condensed milk
Dash of salt
$1/2$ to 1 cup chopped nuts, optional
$1 1/2$ tsp. vanilla extract

Over low heat, melt chips with condensed milk and salt in a heavy saucepan. Remove from heat and stir in nuts and vanilla. Spread evenly into wax paper–lined 8- or 9-inch square pan. Chill for two hours or until firm. Turn fudge onto cutting board, peel off paper, and cut into squares. Store in refrigerator.

CHRISTMAS NATIVITY

History: Nativity scenes were not always small, motionless figurines used for decorating. In fact, the original nativity set was live, with people dressed as Mary and Joseph and real animals used in the barn. Tradition says that the first of these live nativities was created by St. Francis of Assisi in the twelfth century. He is said to have built a manger or crib, added hay, an ox, and a donkey. Once he had recreated the scene, it is said that he stood before the manger, bathed in tears and overflowing with joy.

Most nativity sets contain the three wise men, the shepherd, the star, some sheep, donkeys and cows, a manger with the baby Jesus, Joseph, and Mary.

Typically, the sets were displayed at the front of medieval churches and temples. Eventually, artists began carving these images into wood or making them out of straw, and when the nativity sets moved to other countries like Italy, other materials were used such as stone and ivory. The clothing worn by the wise men changed with the styles adopted by kings of the day, but the shepherds changed very little in regard to dress. In the seventeenth century, the angels were given powdered wigs and hats trimmed with feathers.

Many Italians commissioned the work of famous artists to hand carve and create their nativity scenes. In Rome, a large nativity scene is put out in the square of the Vatican just before Christmas, where many believers come to see its beauty.

When the town of Bethlehem, Pennsylvania, was settled in America in the year 1741, the people there brought this old tradition to the United States. These nativity sets in America were called crèche, which means "crib" in French. The materials used to make modern nativities can range from papier-mâché to glass, resin, or ceramic. Many people choose a barnlike container as the background, while others prefer simpler, more natural backdrops such as rocks or grass.

The nativity story is more than a Christmas story. It provides the foundation for the Christian faith—God sending His Son in human form to tell us about the heavenly Father, give His life for our sins, and reconcile us to Him forever. It simply cannot be told often enough. Christ incarnate, who is the Hope of Glory.

Christmas Idea: A nativity scene is a wonderful way to demonstrate the real meaning of Christmas for your children. Leave them out all year and teach your children who the characters are and what part they play in the greatest story ever told. As Christmas approaches they will have a much better grasp on the meaning behind the season. You might even buy a sturdy nativity that can be used in a nativity play. It need only be big enough to move about.

Christmas Idea: Nativities make a wonderful Christmas gift, and they are often inexpensive. Each year give a new nativity piece to each of your daughters and daughters-in-law. They will enjoy adding to their collections and can pass them down to their daughters and granddaughters.

Christmas Idea: Produce a nativity play for the children in your neighborhood. Work with your children to assign parts, make costumes, and build the props. Use a modern version of the Bible for the narrative. Serve punch and cookies after the play.

Necktie Wreath and Ornaments

For the wreath you will need:

1 14-inch foam wreath form (outside dimension)

15 neckties (or scraps of similar fabrics)

Straight pins

Wire

Wrap the first necktie around the wreath form, starting with the small end of the tie and working it so that the point of the wide end of the tie is pointing outward from the center of the wreath. Use a straight pin to secure the tie in place. Begin the next tie in the same way, overlapping the first by one inch. Secure it with a straight pin and continue until all but one of the ties has been secured to the wreath form.

Wrap a one-foot piece of wire around the top of the wreath to serve as a hanger. Tie the last necktie in a bow around the top to disguise the wire.

For the ornaments you will need:

Assorted neckties or similar fabric scraps

Foam balls

Self-adhesive gold braid

Gold ribbon

Fabric glue

Cut neckties into long, narrow, oval-shaped strips long enough to cover foam balls from top to bottom. Appliqué fabric to foam balls using pins and fabric glue. Cover overlaps between fabric pieces with lengths of gold braid. Attach bows of ribbon to the top of each ball with straight pins; add a U-shaped loop of wire or a hairpin to the top of each ball for hanging.

Homemade Gift Idea for Kids

Kids love homemade gifts, especially if they can eat them. You will need white plastic spoons, a candy cane, a large candy bar, a plastic bag, waxed paper, and a rolling pin. Break up the candy bar and melt it in the microwave. Put the candy cane in the plastic bag and crush it with the rolling pin into fine pieces. Dip the plastic spoons into the melted chocolate bar, filling the curved portion and coating the rest. Hold each spoon for a minute so it can set up and then sprinkle it with candy cane bits and lay it on the waxed paper. When they are cool and hard, cover the top of each one with plastic wrap and anchor it with a small, decorative ribbon.

Outdoor Decorating Idea

Decorate an additional Christmas tree—such as a fir tree growing in your yard. Adorn the tree with wrapped mint candies, bead garlands, and candy canes. Add a sturdy golden star at the top of the tree.

Santa Stats

Weight of Santa's sleigh loaded with one Beanie Baby for every kid on earth: 333,333 tons. Number of reindeer required to pull a 333,333-ton sleigh: 214,206 plus Rudolph.

HARK! THE HERALD ANGELS SING

CHARLES WESLEY

Hark! The herald angels sing,
"Glory to the newborn King!
Peace on earth, and mercy mild,
God and sinners reconciled."
Joyful, all ye nations, rise,
Join the triumph of the skies;
With th' angelic host proclaim,
"Christ is born in Bethlehem."
Hark! The herald angels sing,
"Glory to the newborn King!"

Christ, by highest heav'n adored:
Christ, the everlasting Lord;
Late in time behold Him come,
Offspring of the favored one.
Veil'd in flesh, the Godhead see;
Hail, th' incarnate Deity:
Pleased, as man, with men to dwell,
Jesus, our Emmanuel!
Hark! The herald angels sing,
"Glory to the newborn King!"

Hail! The heav'n-born Prince of Peace!
Hail! The Son of Righteousness!
Light and life to all He brings,

Risen with healing in His wings
Mild He lays His glory by,
Born that man no more may die:
Born to raise the sons of earth,
Born to give them second birth.
Hark! The herald angels sing,
"Glory to the newborn King!"

HISTORICAL NOTE:

When Charles Wesley wrote this beautiful hymn in 1737, it was titled, "Hark! How All the Welkin Rings." A controversy sprang up when George Whitefield, a friend of Wesley's, changed the words of the song to "Hark! the Herald Angels Sing" without the author's permission. When Wesley saw the published work, he was incensed.

Whitefield failed to understand that the biblical account does not mention angels singing. Though it was an angel who made the announcement to the shepherds, the singers were described as a "great heavenly host." These were the creatures referred to by Wesley as the "Welkin." The mistake was insignificant to Whitefield but not to the theologically impeccable Wesley. Tradition says that he never sang the song again.

Ho! Ho! Ho!

If Santa rode a motorcycle what kind would it be?

A Holly Davidson

December 16

WHAT CAN I GIVE HIM?

CHRISTINA ROSSETTI

What can I give Him,
Poor as I am?
If I were a shepherd,
I would bring a lamb.
If I were a wise man,
I would do my part.
Yet what can I give Him?
I give Him my heart.

THE STORY

REBECCA CURRINGTON

*Y*ou know the story—an infant, born in a stable, worshiped by lowly shepherds and travelers from the East. Sweet story, but does it hold any meaning for your life today?

Consider this. The entire Bible pivots on this single event in history. The Old Testament predicts it, and the New Testament confirms it. The child lying in that tiny manger was no ordinary child—He was God incarnate, who came to live and die for you. The story won't be fully told until you bow your knee to Bethlehem's Babe and call Him the Lord of your life. ✶

*There's nothing sadder in this world
than to awake Christmas morning and
not be a child.*

ERMA BOMBECK

CHRISTMAS GIFT IDEAS FOR THE CLERGY

FROM THE BALMY CLERGY SUPPLY
SUBMITTED BY REV. DAVID R. FRANCOEUR

Praying Pants

Research indicates that clergy are the swiftest of all Christians to get down on their knees and pray for the needs of others. As a result, they wear out their pants faster than others. Pants are costly. Therefore Balmy has designed the Praying Pants for durability. The Praying Pants are made of woven Kevlar fiber with air bags on the knees that inflate. Prior to impact a sensor detects the change in the angle of the knee, and a soft cushion of air gently lowers the pastor to a praying position.

XZPP-58 $75.33

Neckband Collar Money Safes

These easy-to-wear neckband collars double as a convenient storage place for folded cash. Thieves may strip you bare and never find your money! Available in all sizes. Intrusion alarm optional.

21V	Box of 3	$25.67
21V-A (with alarm)	Box of 3	$92.10

Early Exit Alarm

Tired of all those people leaving church before the end of the service? A simple laser projector at each door sends out a piercing alarm each time the beam is broken. This splendid device will encourage church members to remain dutifully seated until dismissed.

321-B $2,555.09

Two-Day Clergy Shirt

Designed for the busy pastor or deacon whose schedule won't permit many clothing changes. Reversible design allows for quick change—turning those food stains on the outside to the inside and presenting a fresh-looking replacement. Scotchguarded, this fine shirt resists perspiration.

CC-2	(short sleeve)	$45.92
CC-2A	(long sleeve)	$52.13

Liturgical Aerobics

Now available from Balmy on videotape: Bench Pressing the 1979 Book of Common Prayer by the Rev. Geoffrey Plabbitt, the Episcopal priest who created the concept of "Liturgical Aerobics." A perfect gift for a pastor who is suffering from a lack of exercise.

2196-DJ	$175.99

Stay-Lit Altar Candles

Provide hours of fun as your pastor watches acolytes attempt to extinguish these candles in vain. Developed by the Ecclesial Gag Company.

1429-WM	Box	$56.00

Vacuum-Tube Alms Collection System

Designed to operate like the ones at bank drive-ins. Pew mounted with central receiving station in basement or secured room. Ready to install for 200-pew church. Eliminate the time-consuming offertory.

4715-CL	$103,911.43

Inflatable Congregation

The invention of the century! This device is absolutely perfect for the small church. Make those pews look FULL! One quick twist of the air valve on our patented "Pneuma Tank," and, presto, you have a pew full of excited-looking people. And, for preaching practice, what a marvelous way to finely hone that scintillating sermon by pretending you have a church full of eager parishioners! One (1) air tank comes with order.

6821-ZO $3,329.56

Heavenly Security Systems

The perfect Christmas gift for your pastor! Protect his/her church from burglary with Balmy's Heavenly Security Systems. If a burglar gains entrance to your sanctuary, traditional devices send out a silent alarm to police. Balmy's system does this—and more!

Once the alarm has been tripped, an infrared scanning device locates, tracks, and photographs the thief. The unit then automatically flips on all the interior lights, and a digitized recording of a 250-member choir singing Handel's *Messiah* fills the building with over 170 decibels of sound. Optional features include the Avenging Legion of Angels Holographic Companion to the Messiah, and up to 15 minutes of your pastor's favorite sermon.

3186-HSS $12,995.32

Preaching Gloves and Baptismal Gloves

Another first for Balmy! Genius is as genius does. Here are preaching gloves for your pastor to wear during the winter when the thermostat gets turned down because of budget cutbacks. Also available are baptismal gloves with rubberized tips so that a child won't squirt out of your pastor's hands.

| 62QG-58 | Preaching Gloves | $117.57 |
| 29PX-49 | Baptismal Gloves | $98.33 |

Balmy's Robot Pastor

Japanese Buddhists reportedly have unveiled a "robot priest" which is computer-programmed to perform a variety of rituals. Not to be out-done, Balmy Clergy Supply introduces the Balmy Robot Pastor, which can be used by churches as temporary replacements for vacationing or ill pastors. The Robot Pastor is programmed to identify heretics and church members who have fallen behind on their pledges, and to sound a full-scale trumpet blast when one is identified.

The cost of each Balmy Robot Pastor is the result of a lengthy, heart-felt negotiation between the Balmy sales representative and the church board.[7]

Did You Know?

When Robert Louis Stevenson, author of *Treasure Island*, died on December 4, 1894, he willed his November 13 birthday to a friend who disliked her own Christmas birthday.

Santa Claus has the right idea.
Visit people once a year.

VICTOR BORGE

Edible Holiday Candles

    2 bananas
    4 sugar cookies
    4 maraschino cherries
    4 slices of canned pineapple
    4 tsp. of whipped cream

Place one sugar cookie on each plate. Lay a pineapple slice on top of each cookie. Stand half a banana in the hole of each pineapple. Top the banana with a bit of whipped cream and a cherry.

CHRISTMAS SNOWBALLS

4 sticks butter, melted
2 tsp. vanilla extract
2 cups finely chopped pecans
6 Tbsp. confectioners' sugar
4 cups all-purpose flour
Confectioners' sugar (to roll
  cookies in after baked)

Preheat oven to 325°F.

Mix first 5 ingredients well. Form into 1-inch balls.
Place on ungreased cookie sheet. Bake for 10 to 20
minutes until cookies turn lightly brown. Remove from
oven; cool for 5 minutes. Roll each cookie in confectioners' sugar.

When cool, roll again until well coated. If cookies
break up while rolling in sugar, cool for another
5 minutes. Makes about 100 cookies.

THIS STUPENDOUS STRANGER

CHRISTOPHER SMART

Where is this stupendous stranger?
Prophets, shepherds, kings, advise;
Lead me to my Master's manger,
Show me where my Savior lies.
O most mighty, O most holy,
Far beyond the seraph's thought,
Art thou then so mean and lowly
As unheeded prophets taught?
O the magnitude of meekness,
Worth from worth immortal spring,
O the strength of infant weakness,
If eternal is so young.
God all bounteous, all creative,
Whom no ills from good dissuade,
Is incarnate, and a native
Of the very word he made.

Santa Stats
In the U.S., there are seventy-eight people registered under the name
S. Claus and one under Kris Kringle.

A SHEPHERD

HEYWOOD BROUN

*T*he host of heaven and the angel of the Lord had filled the sky with radiance. Now the glory of God was gone and the shepherds and the sheep stood under dim starlight. The men were shaken by the wonders they had seen and heard and, like the animals, they huddled close.

"Let us now," said the eldest of the shepherds, "go even unto Bethlehem, and see this thing which has come to pass, which the Lord hath made known unto us."

The City of David lay beyond a far, high hill upon the crest of which there danced a star. Then men made haste to be away, but as they broke out of the circle there was one called Amos who remained. He dug his crook into the turf and clung to it.

"Come," cried the eldest of the shepherds, but Amos shook his head. They marveled, and one called out, "It is true. It was an angel. You heard the tidings. A Savior is born!"

"I heard," said Amos. "I will abide."

The eldest walked back from the road to the little knoll on which Amos stood.

"You do not understand," the old man told him. "We have a sign from God. An angel commanded us. We go to worship the Savior, who is even now born in Bethlehem. God has made His will manifest."

"It is not in my heart," replied Amos.

And now the eldest of the shepherds was angry.

"With your own eyes," he cried out, "you have seen the host of heaven in these dark hills. And you heard, for it was like the thunder when 'Glory to God in the highest' came ringing to us out of the night."

And again Amos said, "It is not in my heart."

Another shepherd then broke in. "Because the hills still stand and the sky has not fallen, it is not enough for Amos. He must have something louder than the voice of God."

Amos held more tightly to his crook and answered, "I have need of a whisper."

They laughed at him and said, "What should this voice say in your ear?"

He was silent, and they pressed about him and shouted mockingly, "Tell us now. What says the God of Amos, the little shepherd of a hundred sheep?"

Meekness fell away from him. He took his hands from off the crook and raised them high.

"I too am a god," said Amos in a loud, strange voice, "and to my hundred sheep I am a savior."

And when the din of the angry shepherds about him slackened, Amos pointed to his hundred.

"See my flock," he said. "See the fright of them. The fear of the bright angel and of the voices is still upon them. God is busy in Bethlehem. He has not time for a hundred sheep. They are my sheep. I will abide."

This the others did not take so much amiss, for they saw that there was a terror in all the flocks and they too knew the ways of sheep. And before the shepherds departed on the road to Bethlehem toward the bright star, each talked to Amos and told him what he should do for the care of the several flocks. And yet one or two turned back a moment to taunt Amos, before they reached the dip in the road which led to the City of David. It was said, "We shall see new glories at the throne of God, and you, Amos, you will see sheep."

Amos paid no heed, for he thought to himself, "One shepherd the less will not matter at the throne of God." Nor did he have time to be troubled that he was not to see the Child who was come to save the world. There was much to be done among the flocks, and Amos walked between the sheep and made under his tongue a clucking noise, which was a way he had, and to his hundred and to the others it was a sound more fine and friendly than the voice of the bright angel. Presently the animals ceased to tremble and they began to graze as the sun came up over the hill where the star had been.

"For sheep," said Amos to himself, "the angels shine too much. A shepherd is better."

With the morning the others came up the road from Bethlehem, and they told Amos of the manger and of the wise men who had mingled there with shepherds. And they described to him the gifts: gold, frankincense, and myrrh. And when they were done they said, "And did you see wonders here in the fields with the sheep?"

Amos told them, "Now my hundred are one hundred and one," and he showed them a lamb which had been born just before the dawn.

"Was there for this a great voice out of heaven?" asked the eldest of the shepherds.

Amos shook his head and smiled, and there was upon his face that which seemed to the shepherds a wonder even in a night of wonders.

"To my heart," he said, "there came a whisper."✶

HEYWOOD BROUN (1888–1939)

Journalist and author, Broun was born in Brooklyn and became one of the most widely read newspaper columnists in the U.S. in the early 1900s. After joining the staff of the *New York Tribune*, he began his column, "It Seems to Me."

December 17

*Christmas is not a day or a season, but a condition of heart
and mind. If we love our neighbors as ourselves;
if in our riches we are poor in spirit and in our
poverty we are rich in grace; if our charity vaunts not itself,
but suffers long and is kind; if when our brother asks for a loaf
we give ourselves instead; if each day dawns in opportunity and
sets in achievement, however small; then every day is
Christ's day and Christmas is always near.*

JAMES WALLINGFORD

Why the Chimes Rang

Raymond Macdonald Alden

There was once, in a far-away country where few people have ever traveled, a wonderful church. It stood on a high hill in the midst of a great city; and every Sunday, as well as on sacred days like Christmas, thousands of people climbed the hill to its great archways, looking like lines of ants all moving in the same direction.

When you came to the building itself, you found stone columns and dark passages, and a grand entrance leading to the main room of the church. This room was so long that one standing at the doorway could scarcely see to the other end, where the choir stood by the marble altar. In the farthest corner was the organ; and this organ was so loud that sometimes when it played, the people for miles around would close their shutters and prepare for a great thunderstorm. Altogether, no such church as this was ever seen before, especially when it was lighted up for some festival, and crowded with people, young and old.

But the strangest thing about the whole building was the wonderful chime of bells. At one corner of the church was a great gray tower, with ivy growing over it as far up as one could see. I say as far as one could see, because the tower was quite great enough to fit the great church, and it rose so far into the sky that it was only in very fair weather that any one claimed to be able to see the top. Even then one could not be certain that it was in sight. Up, and up, and up climbed the stones and the ivy; and, as the men who built the church had been dead for hundreds of years, everyone had forgotten how high the tower was supposed to be.

Now all the people knew that at the top of the tower was a chime of Christmas bells. They had hung there ever since the church had been built, and were the most beautiful bells in the world. Some thought it was because a great musician had cast them and arranged them in their place; others said it was because of the great height, which reached up where the air was clearest and purest: however that might be, no one who had ever heard the chimes denied that they were the sweetest in the world. Some described them as sounding like angels far up in the sky; others, as sounding like strange winds singing through the trees.

But the fact was that no one had heard them for years and years. There was an old man living not far from the church, who said that his mother had spoken of hearing them when she was a little girl, and he was the only one who was sure of as much as that. They were Christmas chimes, you see, and were not meant to be played by men or on common days. It was the custom on Christmas Eve for all the people to bring to the church their offerings to the Christ-child; and when the greatest and best offering was laid on the altar, there used to come sounding through the music of the choir the Christmas chimes far up in the tower. Some said that the wind rang them, and others that they were so high that the angels could set them swinging. But for many long years they had never been heard.

It was said that people had been growing less careful of their gifts for the Christ-child, and that no offering was brought great enough to deserve the music of the chimes. Every Christmas Eve the rich people still crowded to the altar, each one trying to bring some better gift than any other, without giving anything that he wanted for himself, and the church was crowded with those who thought that perhaps the wonderful bells might be heard again. But although the service was splendid, and the offerings plenty, only the roar of the wind could be heard, far up in the stone tower.

Now, a number of miles from the city, in a little country village, where nothing could be seen of the great church but glimpses of the tower when the weather was fine, lived a boy named Pedro, and his little brother. They knew very little about the Christmas chimes, but they had heard of the service in the church on Christmas Eve, and had a secret plan, which they had often talked over when by themselves. They would go to see the beautiful celebration.

"Nobody can guess, Little Brother," Pedro would say, "all the fine things there are to see and hear; and I have even heard it said that the Christ-child sometimes comes down to bless the service. What if we could see Him?"

The day before Christmas was bitterly cold, with a few lonely snowflakes flying in the air, and a hard white crust on the ground. Sure enough, Pedro and Little Brother were able to slip quietly away early in the afternoon; and although the walking was hard in the frosty air, before nightfall they had trudged so far, hand in hand, that they saw the lights of the big city just ahead of them. Indeed, they were about to enter one of the great gates in the wall that surrounded it, when they saw something dark on the snow near their path, and stepped aside to look at it.

It was a poor woman who had fallen just outside the city, too sick and tired to get in where she might have found shelter. The soft snow made of a drift a sort of pillow for her, and she would soon be so sound asleep, in the wintry air, that no one could ever waken her again. All this Pedro saw in a moment, and he knelt down beside her and tried to rouse her, even tugging at her arm a little, as though he would have tried to carry her away. He turned her face toward him, so that he could rub some of the snow on it, and when he had looked at her silently a moment he stood up again, and said: "It's no use, Little Brother. You will have to go on alone."

"Alone?" cried Little Brother. "And you not see the Christmas festival?"

"No," said Pedro, and he could not keep back a bit of a choking sound in his throat. "See this poor woman. Her face looks like the Madonna in the chapel window, and she will freeze to death if nobody cares for her. Every one has gone to the church now, but when you come back you can bring some one to help her. I will rub her to keep her from freezing, and perhaps get her to eat the bun that is left in my pocket."

"But I cannot bear to leave you, and go on alone," said Little Brother.

"Both of us need not miss the service," said Pedro, "and it had better be I than you. You can easily find your way to the church; and you must see and hear everything twice, Little Brother—once for you and once for me. I am sure the Christ-child must know how I should love to come with you and worship Him; and oh! if you get a chance, Little Brother, to slip up to the altar without getting in any one's way, take this little silver piece of mine, and lay it down for my offering, when no one is looking. Do not forget where you have left me, and forgive me for not going with you."

In this way he hurried Little Brother off to the city, and winked hard to keep back the tears, as he heard the crunching footsteps sounding farther and farther away in the twilight. It was pretty hard to lose the music and splendor of the Christmas celebration that he had been planning for so long, and spend the time instead in that lonely place in the snow.

The great church was a wonderful place that night. Every one said that it had never looked so bright and beautiful before. When the organ played and the thousands of people sang, the walls shook with the sound, and little Pedro, away outside the city wall, felt the earth tremble around him.

At the close of the service came the procession with the offerings to be laid on the altar. Rich men and great men marched proudly up to lay down their gifts to the Christ-child. Some brought wonderful jewels, some baskets of gold so heavy that they could scarcely carry them down the aisle. A great writer laid down a book that he had been making for years and years. And last of all walked the king of the country, hoping with all the rest to win for himself the chime of the Christmas bells. There went a great murmur through the church, as the people saw the king take from his head the royal crown, all set with precious stones, and lay it gleaming on the altar, as his offering to the holy Child. "Surely," every one said, "we shall hear the bells now, for nothing like this has ever happened before."

But still only the cold old wind was heard in the tower, and the people shook their heads; and some of them said, as they had before, that they never really believed the story of the chimes, and doubted if they ever rang at all.

The procession was over, and the choir began the closing hymn. Suddenly the organist stopped playing as though he had been shot, and every one looked at the old minister, who was standing by the altar, holding up his hand for silence. Not a sound could be heard from any one in the church, but as all the people strained their ears to listen, there came softly, but distinctly, swinging through the air, the sound of the chimes in the tower. So far away, and yet so clear the music seemed—so much sweeter were the notes than anything that had been heard before, rising and falling away up there in the sky, that the people in the church sat for a moment as still as though something held each of them by the shoulders. Then they all stood up together and stared straight at the altar, to see what great gift had awakened the long-silent bells.

But all that the nearest of them saw was the childish figure of Little Brother, who had crept softly down the aisle when no one was looking, and had laid Pedro's little piece of silver on the altar. ✳

RAYMOND MACDONALD ALDEN (1873–1924)
An American scholar and educator, the author of this story was born in New Hartford, New York, and began writing as a child. His mother was the author of the Pansy Books, a type of religious Sunday-school fiction widely read by young people. Alden wrote this story for the Pansy Books one Christmas season at her request. Alden went on to become the head of the English Department at Stanford University—and his story has been a favorite of generations of young readers.

CHRISTMAS DINNER IN BULGARIA

Traditional Bulgarian Menu

Cabbage Sarmi (cabbage leaves stuffed with rice or beans)

Stuffed peppers

Turshia (pickles)

Oshav (boiled dried fruit)

Beans

Walnuts

Apples

Honey

Bread

The History

- The month before Christmas is considered a time of fasting in antici-pation of the celebration of Christ. Christmas Eve is the last day of the fast—which prohibits the eating of meat.
- Most, if not all, of the traditional Christmas activities take place on Christmas Eve rather than Christmas Day, including the family din-ner.
- Christmas dinner consists of at least twelve dishes—all meatless.
- The main dish is a huge round bread, with pictures of houses and cattle—whatever represents wealth—carved on the crust.
- The father of the family moves through the house with incense before the family takes their places at the table.
- The meal begins with garlic to ensure good health for the coming year.
- Bread and honey follow to ensure that the coming year will be sweet.
- Christmas bread is an important dinner ritual. The oldest member of

the family takes three pieces of bread and sets them aside, one for the Christ Child, one for Mary, and the other for the household. He then breaks up the bread and gives a piece to everyone at the table.

- Straw is used for decorations to symbolize the straw in the stable at Bethlehem. It is typically placed on the table under a white tablecloth.

- Traditionally, boys and unmarried men traveled around the neighborhood wishing the home owners good health and prosperity for which they received gifts of food and money.

Did You Know?

- No one is to stand up until the entire meal is finished.
- The round bread contains a small coin. The tradition is the person who gets the coin will be the luckiest in the upcoming year.
- Turshia is made of vegetables such as carrots, cucumbers, cauliflower, small peppers, garlic, and celery, tinned in a special sauce of vinegar, oil, and salt.

For Our Bulgarian Friends: May your walnuts be tasty and delicious! After the meal, everyone is given a walnut to open. If the meat of the walnut is good and delicious, the year will be prosperous. If the walnut is empty—oops, not good news—reach for another walnut!

Christmas is the day that holds all time together.
ALEXANDER SMITH

GINGERSNAPS

3/4 cup vegetable shortening

1 cup sugar

1 egg

1/4 tsp. salt

4 Tbsp. molasses

2 cups all-purpose flour

3 tsp. baking soda

1 tsp. ginger

1 tsp. cinnamon

1/2 tsp. ground cloves

Preheat oven to 350°F.

In a large bowl, cream together the shortening and sugar with mixer on medium, until light. Add the egg, salt, and molasses; mix well. In a separate bowl, sift together the next 5 ingredients. Slowly blend into the creamed mixture a little at a time. Form dough into small balls; roll in sugar. Place on a greased cookie sheet. Bake for 10 to 12 minutes or until lightly brown.

Tip: For crunchier snaps, flatten ball with the bottom of glass before baking.

Did You Know?

Mince pies were once shaped like mangers and are thought to date back to the sweetmeats formerly presented to the Vatican on Christmas Eve.

～

Gift Idea for Romantics

Nothing says romance like champagne and chocolate. Plan a quiet little celebration for just the two of you. Bring a box of exquisite chocolates and a bottle of bubbly. You might prefer to invest in chocolate-covered strawberries—they can be purchased online.

～

Santa's Christmas Advice:

- Encourage people to believe in you.
- Always remember who's naughty and who's nice.
- Don't pout.
- It's as much fun to give as it is to receive.
- Some days it's okay to feel a little chubby.
- Make your presents known.
- Always ask for a little bit more than what you really want.
- Bright red can make anyone look good.
- Wear a wide belt and no one will notice how many pounds you've gained.
- If you only show up once a year, everyone will think you're very important.
- Whenever you're at a loss for words, say: "HO, HO, HO!"

CHRISTMAS CAROLING

History: A Christmas carol, also called a noel, is a song or hymn whose lyrics are on the theme of Christmas or the winter season in general. These hail back as far as the thirteenth century. Although carols were originally communal songs sung during celebrations like harvest tide, it was only later that carols began to be sung in church, and to be specifically associated with Christmas.

A popular urban legend has it that these songs and hymns were named carols after a little girl named Carol Poles who disappeared in 1888 in the Whitechapel district of London around Christmastime. Groups of searchers were knocking on doors at night to ask if residents had seen the child. They received little help, however, because residents, frightened by the reports of Jack the Ripper, refused to open their doors and answer questions. To alleviate their fears, the groups would sing Christmas songs to let the people inside know they were friendly.

Traditional carols have a strong tune and consist of a verse and/or chorus for group singing. They are often based on medieval chord patterns, and it is this that gives them their uniquely characteristic musical sound.

It is said that Saint Francis of Assisi first introduced carols into a church service during a Christmas Midnight Mass in Greccio, in the province of Umbria in 1223.

Most Christmas carols tell a story, usually about some triumphant aspect of the birth of Christ. Church music of the time was solemn, even mournful, so these carols provided an opportunity for churchgoers to express their feelings of joy and happiness.

In some countries—notably England, America, Poland, and Bulgaria—Christmas caroling is still a popular Christmas activity. Groups of carolers are often rewarded with money (to be given to charity), Christmas treats, and warm drinks. Australia's caroling tradition is somewhat different. Since it comes in the middle of summer, carolers sing at outdoor concerts called Carols by Candlelight. These take place in cities and towns across Australia during the weeks leading up to Christmas Day. Melbourne has the largest production always held on Christmas Eve. This grand event includes opera singers, musical theater performers, and popular singers. Audience members hold up lit candles and join in the singing of the carols.

Christmas Idea: The week before Christmas, invite your neighbors to go caroling with you and your family. Just after dark, go from house to house singing carols. It's best to stand in the driveway or even on the street since people are particular about their lawns. Sing just one or two songs before moving on to the next house. When you get back, invite everyone in for hot chocolate and cookies.

Christmas Idea: Recruit a group of carolers from your neighborhood or church and visit a nursing home or facility for the elderly. You will need to obtain permission from the facility before doing this. Ask to sing in the lobby or just outside on the parking lot or lawn. From there the residents can see and hear you from their rooms. Bring along small gifts or flowers and let the children in the group hand them out to the residents.

CHOCOLATE HAYSTACK CHRISTMAS COOKIES

6 ounces chocolate chips
6 ounces butterscotch chips
6 ounces chow mein noodles (dry)

Melt chocolate and butterscotch chips together in double boiler. Blend together thoroughly. Stir in noodles until mixture becomes stiff enough to spoon out. Drop by tsp. onto waxed paper. Refrigerate until hard.

Kissing Ball

1 large potato

Loop of strong but flexible wire (such as a wire coat hanger)

A small bunch of greenery (boxwood or cedar, for example)

Floral picks

Ribbon for a bow

Small nuts, pine cones, or berries

Choose a large, firm potato; then push a loop of wire through the bottom of the potato in two places. Twist the ends of the wire together at the top.

Wire several sprigs of greenery together on a floral pick to form a full bunch and insert the pick into the base of the potato.

Cover the potato completely with greenery, forming a full ball. To maintain the round shape, trim any sprigs that are uneven. Decorate the top of the ball with nuts, pine cones, or berries wired to a floral pick. Wrap the wire loop at the top with ribbon, leaving a long strip for hanging. Finish with a bow.

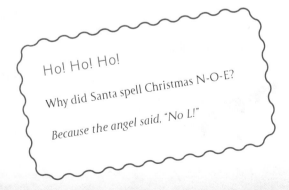

Ho! Ho! Ho!

Why did Santa spell Christmas N-O-E?

Because the angel said, "No L!"

JINGLE BELLS

James Pierpont

Dashing through the snow in a one-horse open sleigh,
Over the fields we go, laughing all the way;
Bells on bob-tail ring, making spirits bright,
What fun it is to ride and sing a sleighing song tonight.
Jingle bells, jingle bells,
Jingle all the way!
O what fun it is to ride
In a one-horse open sleigh.

A day or two ago, the story I must tell
I went out on the snow and on my back I fell;
A gent was riding by in a one-horse open sleigh,
He laughed as there I sprawling lie, but quickly drove away.
Jingle Bells, Jingle Bells,
Jingle all the way!
O what fun it is to ride
In a one-horse open sleigh.

Now the ground is white, so do it while you're young.
Take the girls tonight and sing this sleighing song;
Just get a bob-tailed bay two-forty as his speed
Hitch him to an open sleigh and crack! you'll take the lead.
Jingle Bells, Jingle Bells,
Jingle all the way!
O what fun it is to ride
In a one-horse open sleigh.

HISTORICAL NOTE:

Originally known as "One-Horse Open Sleigh," this Christmas favorite is the best-known and most commonly sung secular Christmas song in the world. The author wrote it in 1857 for a Thanksgiving program at his church in Savannah, Georgia. In its original version, the song had a different melody for the chorus—less joyous and more classical sounding. It is unknown who replaced the original with the modern version we know today.

"Jingle Bells" was the first song broadcast from space in a Christmas-themed prank by Gemini 6 astronauts Tom Stafford and Wally Schirra on December 16, 1965. They contacted Mission Control with a report:

"We have an object, looks like a satellite going from north to south, probably in polar orbit... I see a command module and eight smaller modules in front. The pilot of the command module is wearing a red suit..."

The astronauts then produced a smuggled harmonica and sleigh bells and broadcast a rendition of "Jingle Bells."[8]

Who Brings the Gifts?

Santa doesn't bring the gifts in these countries:

- Spain and South America: The Three Kings
- England: Father Christmas
- France: Père Noël (Father Christmas)
- Russia: Babouschka (a grandmotherly figure) or Grandfather Frost.
- Holland: St. Nicholas

Did You Know?

According to a survey, seven out of ten British dogs get Christmas gifts from their doting owners.

December 18

MUCH MORE TO CHRISTMAS

AUTHOR UNKNOWN

There's more, much more to Christmas
Than candlelight and cheer;
It's the spirit of sweet friendship,
That brightens all the year;
It's thoughtfulness and kindness,
It's hope reborn again,
For peace, for understanding
And for goodwill to men!

HARRY THE SINGING ANGEL

ROBERT PENGOLD

*H*arry wasn't all that upset at the beginning. After all, he had been a singing angel last year, as opposed to a "hovering" angel. The hovering angels were only two and three years old. They didn't say a word. They just stood at the front and looked good. Singing angels were four, five, and six, and Harry was five years old—"mature for his age," he had heard people say.

It was far better to be a singing angel, Harry had concluded last year, since singing angels didn't have to wear those weird halos or fancy wings—the wings of the singing angels were part of the collar of the costume. And...the song was pretty simple to sing—not a bad song as songs go. "Hark, the herald angels sing, glory to the newborn king, peace on earth and mercy mild, God and sinner reconciled." He had the words down cold, although he still had a little question about just exactly what "mercy mild" was all about.

Harry's older brother, Billy, was eight years old, and he was going to be a shepherd—also for the second time. Both Harry and Billy had their costumes, which only needed to be lengthened a little at the sleeves and hem. Grandma had finished hemming them even before the first rehearsal.

Yep, it was looking like a pretty routine Christmas program. "No big deal," Harry told himself.

That is, until the announcement came—the announcement about who was going to play the part of Baby Jesus.

Harry was not amused. Somebody—somebody totally out of their minds, he concluded—had decided that Baby Jesus was going to be played by Baby Tommy. *His* Baby Tommy. Not an anonymous new baby in the church...or a new kid on the block...but the new kid in the crib in the room next to his room at his house. Baby Tommy, Harry's little brother.

It wasn't that Harry didn't like Baby Tommy, or even love him. At least he never could have admitted it. Mom would have had a fit.

Harry wasn't sure exactly *what* he felt. He knew that in the beginning he had been very excited about having a baby in the house. It was all he had talked about for months. Everybody had said he was taking Mom's pregnancy all in stride. A baby had been welcome news.

Harry had been sure that with the arrival of a new baby, he would no longer have to bear the title of "little brother." He finally was going to be somebody's "big brother"—and that had a pretty cool ring to it. Mom had assured him that he didn't have to give up his bed or his room—he didn't even have to share his room, at least for a while, she said.

Dad had talked about how much fun it would be to have three kids instead of just two, and Harry could see some advantages in that, too. Maybe with a baby brother or sister around, *he* wouldn't always be blamed when something broke or something went wrong. He was certain he could out-run, out-argue, and out-yell any baby. It might be nice to have somebody to boss around...just like Billy bossed him around.

All in all, it was no-o-o-o problem. Harry was excited about having a baby in the family. That is...until Baby Tommy actually showed up.

From the best Harry could tell, Baby Tommy appeared to have taken over.

When Baby Tommy cried...both Mom and Dad jumped. Mom didn't seem very patient with Billy or Harry these days...but when Baby Tommy needed a diaper change or to be fed, Mom was all smiles and lovey-dovey. Dad didn't seem to have as much time to play ball as he did before Baby Tommy arrived...but he *always* seemed to find time when he got home to pick up Baby Tommy and cuddle *him*.

And...it was pretty amazing all the things Mom and Dad both expected Harry to do now. Why, they expected him to be able to dress himself *completely*, even to tying real shoelaces, and to put his own dirty clothes in the hamper, and to smooth out his bed before kindergarten started. He had never had to do any of those things before Baby Tommy arrived. And not only that, but he had to carry his own dishes to the kitchen sink from the table and worst of all, he had to sit in the *middle* of the backseat. There went the window view.

To top it all off, neither Mom nor Dad had been very amused when Harry had suggested that maybe—just *maybe*—they might be able to trade in Baby Tommy on a baby that cried a little less. It was only a suggestion—he didn't see why everybody got *that* upset. It certainly didn't seem to be worth a time out and no dessert.

No, all in all, Baby Tommy had been a much better "idea" than a reality. And now...to have Baby Tommy as the *star* of the Christmas program...to have Baby Tommy playing Baby Jesus...well that was just too much to ask, even of a singing angel.

Mom had insisted that Harry go to practices and walk through the motions. Dad had backed up her order with that "look" of his. *But*, Harry decided all on his own, *nobody could make him sing*.

"Glory to the newborn king?" Yeah, right. He wasn't about to call Baby Tommy a newborn king—Dad was already calling him a "little prince" and that was far enough in the line of royalty.

Nope...Harry may not be able to boycott the entire Christmas program, but he certainly didn't have to sing. Of that he was not only certain, but determined. It would be his little secret and that was that. No singing for Harry *this* year.

He almost gave in when Miss Martin came to talk to him about sing-ing. Miss Martin was his kindergarten Sunday school teacher, and besides Mom and Aunt Carla, she was the prettiest and nicest woman Harry had ever met. He had even thought that he might like to marry her someday, maybe after first grade. Miss Martin told great Bible stories—why, she even made some of those people in the Bible seem *real*. He liked Daniel a lot. It *would* have been scary to be thrown into a lion's den. Miss Martin seemed to understand that. And it would have been pretty gross to be in the belly of a whale like Jonah—Miss Martin sometimes used words like gross. And he especially liked what Miss Martin had to say about Jesus, and about how He healed people and did miracles and all.

Perhaps the *very* best thing about Miss Martin, though, was that she treated Harry—why, as if he was at least six years old, maybe even seven. She always called him "Harold," which had a very grown-up ring to it as far as Harry was concerned. That was his real name, of course, Harold Reginald Loveless. (But don't tell anybody about that name Reginald.) His older brother was William Samuel Loveless...Billy for short. And Baby Tommy was really named Thomas—well, Thomas *something* Loveless. Harry didn't like it when most people called him Harold, but with Miss Martin it was OK.

Miss Martin had come to him, asking in a very nice voice, "Harold, do you have a sore throat?"

"No, Miss Martin," he had replied.

"Well, I've noticed you aren't singing. You have such a nice, strong voice for a boy, and you always sing in tune and know all the words. We really need you to sing out *strong*, Harold. We can't do this very well without you!"

Harry had just looked down. He really didn't want to give Miss Martin any reason to dislike him, but he was determined *not* to sing if Baby Tommy was going to be Baby Jesus.

"Is something the matter?" Miss Martin had asked.

"No, Ma'am," Harry had said.

"Well," Miss Martin said, "I know you know the words and you know the tune, so I believe that when the time comes, you'll be the best singing angel up there."

Harry really was pretty sorry that Miss Martin was going to be disappointed. But this year, it just couldn't be helped. He had one more year of being a singing angel ahead of him, and she would just have to wait until then. He had no doubt he *could* be the best singing angel...but not this year.

The days passed. Rehearsals came and went. Harry hoped against hope that another baby would be born or somebody else would be chosen to be Baby Jesus. He had even hoped in secret that Baby Tommy would get sick so they'd *have* to find another Baby Jesus. No such luck.

If anything, as the days went by, Tommy just got more and more attention, and became more and more demanding. Why, they even had a party for Baby Tommy and he got all kinds of gifts—it wasn't even Christmas or his birthday or *anything*. And it seemed everybody in the whole world had been by the house to oooh and aaah over Baby Tommy. They didn't even seem to notice Harry most of the time. It wasn't fair.

Certainly nothing had happened to change Harry's mind. He was determined more than ever to carry out his plan, even if nobody ever knew about it. He'd know, and that's all that mattered. There would be no singing from Harry Loveless' lips this year.

The evening of the Christmas program finally showed up, and so did Baby Tommy bundled in a soft white blanket. Mom helped Billy with the headdress he had to wear as a shepherd and she helped Harry into his singing-angel costume, but mostly she fussed over Baby Tommy, trying to put him to sleep before the show. Harry had to agree that he'd be a lot less trouble asleep than awake.

Miss Martin got everybody lined up in the right order. Then, Reverend Brown showed up to say a prayer and to tell all the angels, "Be sure to sing your best!" Harry pretended not to hear him, which wasn't really all that hard since Clarence Fosdick kept punching him in the ribs. (Even though he was also five years old, it was Clarence's first year as a singing angel and he seemed pretty nervous about it as best Harry could tell.)

Harry walked in like the pro that he was, and when he got up into the choir area, he took his place near the manger. All the kids did pretty good jobs in their speaking parts, he thought—the narrators telling the first part of the story while Mary and Joseph made their way to the choir from the back of the church. Mary was riding a *real* donkey this year! That was a new twist. Harry was pretty impressed, and everybody else seemed to feel the same way. Yeah, this was turning out to be a pretty awesome Christmas program.

The innkeeper did his part, and then Mary and Joseph sang a song and while the spotlight was just on them, a lady dressed all in black brought in Baby Tommy and put him in the manger.

"Baby Jesus, yeah right," Harry said under his breath. He was glad Baby Tommy seemed sound asleep. "He'll never even know he was Baby Jesus," Harry whispered to himself. "And maybe nobody else will."

Then the spotlight went away, and the lights came up, and Mary and Joseph went over and stood by the manger, and Mary kneeled down and started to sing a little lullaby. To Harry's surprise, she reached over and picked up Baby Jesus—that is, Baby Tommy. *Big mistake*, Harry thought to himself. *She's gonna wake him up!*

And sure enough, Baby Tommy started to whimper. Just a little at first. And then a little more.

Oh no! thought Harry. *He's going to spoil the whole thing.*

Harry glanced out at Mom and Dad on the second row, and he could tell Mom was getting nervous. Dad, too. Billy was at the back of the church waiting to walk in with the shepherds. Harry could tell Baby Tommy was getting ready to wind up with one of his walloping cries—his face was scrunching up for that moment by moment. *What should he do?*

Then Baby Tommy really let loose with a cry. It was huge. In fact, it may have been the biggest baby cry that anybody had every heard in that church. Harry could see the lady dressed in black start toward the back entrance to the choir area. *No!* Harry thought. *You can't have a Christmas program without a Baby Jesus in the manger. It just wouldn't be right. She can't come and take Baby Jesus away.*

Harry had known all along that Baby Tommy wasn't going to be a very good Baby Jesus, but Harry couldn't let Baby Tommy ruin the whole program. He stepped out of line without a glance at Miss Martin—he figured she'd probably be upset with him, but it couldn't be helped. He quickly walked over and knelt down by the manger and stuck out his hand to take Baby Tommy's little fingers.

"It's OK," he said in a very low little voice while Mary went right on with her song. Baby Tommy seemed surprised at another touch and opened his eyes, and Harry leaned over and patted him on the head and whispered, "It's OK. It's OK."

For a few seconds, Baby Tommy stopped whimpering as he seemed to stare up at Harry. Then Harry could see a cry starting to brew again.

Behind him, Harry heard the introduction from the organ for the singing angels song. *Maybe the music will keep him quiet,* Harry thought. But that cry still seemed on the way. What could he do? He had to do something! It wasn't at all what he had planned. But out of Harry's own mouth, he heard a song, "Hark, the herald angels sing"—Baby Tommy seemed to be listening!

Was that a smile? Harry wondered. He wasn't sure he'd ever seen Baby Tommy smile before. "Glory to the newborn king." Yep. Baby Tommy definitely seemed to be listening. "Peace on earth and mercy mild"—Now Baby Tommy was staring all around..."God and sinner reconciled."

Baby Tommy was closing his eyes! *Yeah, that's it.* Harry thought. And Mary, smart woman at last, put Baby Jesus—Baby Tommy, that is—back in the manger. Harry still held onto his hand, though, just in case. "Joyful all ye nations rise. Join the triumph in the skies"...Sure enough, Baby Tommy seemed to be going back to sleep. "With angelic hosts proclaim, Christ is born in Bethlehem." Harry could feel Baby Tommy's fingers loosening their grip, so he let go and stood up to rejoin the choir for the last line. After all he'd sung this much—"Hark, the herald angels sing, glory to the newborn king."

Harry wasn't sure how the rest of the program turned out. He was too busy watching Baby Jesus—that is, Baby Tommy. He guessed that the shepherds did their part OK. Billy didn't say anything later and neither did Mom or Dad, so it must have gone alright. The wise men were a big hit. They didn't come in riding on live camels, but they did have humongous trains on their robes that had the entire audience whispering. All Harry cared about was that Baby Tommy was asleep and that he stayed asleep. Pretty soon it was over.

Backstage, everybody was in a jumble trying to get out of their costumes and find their coats.

Harry was feeling very relieved, and then he saw Miss Martin coming his way. *How could he tell her that he just had to get out of line?*...but before he could get much further in his thinking, Miss Martin gave him a big hug and then got down on his level so she could look him right in the eye.

All she said was, "Hark! The angel Harold sang!"

Yeah, he guessed he had. "Well," Harry said to Miss Martin, "sometimes you just have to help other people act like Jesus."✳

There has been only one Christmas—
the rest are anniversaries.

W. J. CAMERON

THE EMPEROR'S CHRISTMAS CAKE

Ingredients:

1/2 pound butter

1/4 pound white sugar

1 1/4 pound brown sugar

4 eggs

4 Tbsp. brandy

1/2 pound raisins

1/2 pound sultanas

1/2 pound currants

Lemon peel and almonds to taste

10 ounces plain flour

1/2 tsp. baking powder

1 tsp. nutmeg

1 tsp. cinnamon or allspice

Pinch of salt

1 Tbsp. plum jelly

Cream butter and sugar. Add eggs. Sift in half of flour and add half of fruit. Mix. Add the remainder of the ingredients. Bake in an 8-inch pan for 3 1/2 to 4 hours at 300° F.

UP ON THE HOUSETOP

BENJAMIN R. HANBY

Up on the housetop reindeer pause,
Out jumps good ol' Santa Claus.
Down thru' the chimney with lots of toys,
All for the little ones Christmas joys.
Ho, ho, ho! Who wouldn't go!
Ho, ho, ho! Who wouldn't go!
Up on the housetop, click, click, click,
Down thru' the chimney with good Saint Nick.

First comes the stocking of little Nell,
Oh, dear Santa fill it well;
Give her a dolly that laughs and cries
One that will open and shut her eyes.
Ho, ho, ho! Who wouldn't go!
Ho, ho, ho! Who wouldn't go!
Up on the housetop, click, click, click,
Down thru' the chimney with good Saint Nick.

Next comes the stocking of little Will,
Oh just see what a glorious fill
Here is a hammer and lots of tacks,
Also a ball and a whip that cracks.
Ho, ho, ho! Who wouldn't go!
Ho, ho, ho! Who wouldn't go!
Up on the housetop, click, click, click,
Down thru' the chimney with good Saint Nick.

"Up on the Housetop," known as the immortal Christmas song, was first published in 1866 as "Santa Claus." Student, teacher, minister, abolitionist, father, and composer Benjamin Russell Hanby authored numerous songs, but this was his most popular.

Crazy Christmas Signs:

• Toy Store: "Ho, ho, ho spoken here."

• Bridal boutique: "Marry Christmas."

• Outside a church: "The original Christmas Club."

• At a department store: "Big pre-Christmas sale. Come in and mangle with the crowd."

• A reducing salon: "24 Shaping Days until Christmas."

• In a stationery store: "For the man who has everything—a calendar to remind him when payments are due."

Tips for Storing Decorations

Store ornaments and fragile decorations in a box filled with shredded newspaper. This will protect them without having to wrap them separately. Cover the box in brightly colored Christmas wrap so it can be found easily in the attic, on shelves, or in closets.

HOMEMADE CLAY FOR TREE ORNAMENTS

1 cup cornstarch

2 cups baking soda

1 1/2 cups cold water

string

paint

clear shellac

In a saucepan, stir together cornstarch, baking soda, and water. Heat, stirring constantly until mixture reaches a slightly moist, mashed-potato consistency. Pour onto a plate and cover with a damp cloth. When cooled, knead like dough. Roll out to a quarter-inch thickness and cut with a knife or cookie cutter. Pierce a hole near the top for the string. Let dry; paint. When paint is dry, finish with a coat of shellac.

Did You Know?

In an effort to solicit cash to pay for a charity Christmas dinner in 1891, a large crab pot was set down on a San Francisco street, becoming the first Salvation Army collection kettle.

Did You Know?

Cultured Christmas trees must be shaped as they grow to produce fuller foliage. To slow the upward growth and to encourage branching, they are hand-clipped each spring. Trees grown in the wild have sparser branches, and are known in the industry as "Charlie Brown" trees.

A Christmas Tree

Charles Dickens

I have been looking on, this evening, at a merry company of children assembled round that pretty German toy, a Christmas Tree. The tree was planted in the middle of a great round table, and towered high above their heads. It was brilliantly lighted by a multitude of little tapers; and everywhere sparkled and glittered with bright objects.

There were rosy-cheeked dolls, hiding behind green leaves; and there were real watches (with movable hands, at least, and an endless capacity of being wound up) dangling from innumerable twigs; there were French-polished tables, chairs, bedsteads, wardrobes, eight-day clocks, and various other articles of domestic furniture (wonderfully made, in tin, at Wolverhampton), perched among the boughs, as if in preparation for some fairy housekeeping; there were jolly, broad-faced little men, much more agreeable in appearance than many real men—and no wonder, for their heads took off, and showed them to be full of sugar-plums;...there were trinkets for the elder girls, farbrighter than any grown-up gold and jewels; there were baskets and pincushions in all devices; there were guns, swords, and banners;...there were teetotums, humming-tops, needle-cases, pen-wipers, smelling-bottles, conversation-cards, bouquet-holders; real fruit, made artificially dazzling with gold leaf; imitation apples, pears, and walnuts, crammed with surprises; in short, as a pretty child, before me, delightedly whispered to another pretty child, her bosom friend, "There was everything, and more." ✳

You can never truly enjoy Christmas until you can look up into the Father's face and tell Him you have received His Christmas gift.

John R. Rice

December 19

[Jesus said,] "I have come as a light into
the world that whoever believes in Me should
not abide in darkness."
(John 12:46, NKJV)

THE HOLY NIGHT

SELMA LAGERLÖF

*T*here was a man who went out in the dark night to borrow live coals to kindle a fire. He went from hut to hut and knocked. "Dear friends, help me!" said he. "My wife has just given birth to a child, and I must make a fire to warm her and the little one."

But it was way in the night, and all the people were asleep. No one replied.

The man walked and walked. At last he saw the gleam of a fire a long way off. Then he went in that direction, and saw that the fire was burning in the open. A lot of sheep were sleeping around the fire, and an old shepherd sat and watched over the flock.

When the man who wanted to borrow fire came up to the sheep, he saw that three big dogs lay asleep at the shepherd's feet. All three awoke when the man approached and opened their great jaws, as though they wanted to bark; but not a sound was heard. The man noticed that the hair on their backs stood up and that their sharp, white teeth glistened in the firelight. They dashed toward him.

He felt that one of them bit at his leg and one at his hand and that one clung to his throat. But their jaws and teeth wouldn't obey them, and the man didn't suffer the least harm.

Now the man wished to go farther, to get what he needed. But the sheep lay back to back and so close to one another that he couldn't pass them. Then the man stepped upon their backs and walked over them and up to the fire. And not one of the animals awoke or moved.

When the man had almost reached the fire, the shepherd looked up. He was a surly old man, who was unfriendly and harsh toward human beings. And when he saw the strange man coming, he seized the long, spiked staff, which he always held in his hand when he tended his flock, and threw it at him. The staff came right toward the man, but, before it reached him, it turned off to one side and whizzed past him, far out to the meadow.

Now the man came up to the shepherd and said to him: "Good man, help me, and lend me a little fire! My wife has just given birth to a child, and I must make a fire to warm her and the little one."

The shepherd would rather have said no, but when he pondered that the dogs couldn't hurt the man, and the sheep had not run from him, and that the staff had not wished to strike him, he was a little afraid, and dared not deny the man that which he asked.

"Take as much as you need!" he said to the man.

But then the fire was nearly burnt out. There were no logs or branches left, only a big heap of live coals; and the stranger had neither spade nor shovel wherein he could carry the red-hot coals.

When the shepherd saw this, he said again: "Take as much as you need!"

But the man stooped and picked coals from the ashes with his bare hands, and laid them in his mantle. And he didn't burn his hands when he touched them, nor did the coals scorch his mantle; but he carried them away as if they had been nuts or apples.

And when the shepherd, who was such a cruel and hardhearted man, saw all this, he began to wonder to himself: What kind of a night is this, when the dogs do not bite, the sheep are not scared, the staff does not kill, or the fire scorch? He called the stranger back and said to him: "What kind of a night is this? And how does it happen that all things show you compassion?"

Then said the man: "I cannot tell you if you yourself do not see it." And he wished to go his way, that he might soon make a fire and warm his wife and child.

But the shepherd did not wish to lose sight of the man before he had found out what all this might portend. He got up and followed the man till they came to the place where he lived.

Then the shepherd saw that the man didn't have so much as a hut to dwell in, but that his wife and babe were lying in a mountain grotto, where there was nothing except the cold and naked stone walls.

But the shepherd thought that perhaps the poor innocent child might freeze to death there in the grotto; and, although he was a hard man, he was touched, and thought he would like to help it. And he loosened his knapsack from his shoulder, took from it a soft white sheepskin, gave it to the strange man, and said that he should let the child sleep on it.

But just as soon as he showed that he, too, could be merciful, his eyes were opened and he saw what he had not been able to see before, and heard what he could not have heard before.

He saw that all around him stood a ring of little silver-winged angels, and each held a stringed instrument, and all sang in loud tones that tonight the Savior was born who should redeem the world from its sins.

Then he understood how all things were so happy this night that they didn't want to do anything wrong.

And it was not only around the shepherd that there were angels, but he saw them everywhere. They sat inside the grotto, they sat outside on the mountain, and they flew under the heavens. They came marching in great companies, and as they passed, they paused and cast a glance at the child.

There were such jubilation and such gladness and songs and play! And all this he saw in the dark night, whereas before he could not have made out anything. He was so happy because his eyes had been opened that he fell upon his knees and thanked God.

What that shepherd saw, we might also see, for the angels fly down from heaven every Christmas Eve, if we could only see them.

You must remember this, for it is as true, as true as that I see you and you see me. It is not revealed by the light of lamps or candles, and it does not depend upon sun and moon; but that which is needful is that we have such eyes as can see God's glory. ✳

SELMA LAGERLÖF (1858–1940)

A talented Swedish author, Lagerlöf won the Nobel Prize for Literature in 1909. The award read: "in appreciation of the lofty idealism, vivid imagination, and spiritual perception that characterize her writings." She was raised at Marbacka, her family's estate in Sweden, and stayed there until she left for a teacher's college in Stockholm in 1881. In 1885, she became a teacher at a girls' secondary school. A writing competition provided an opportunity for readers to see excerpts from her first, best, and most popular work, "Gosta Berlings Saga." She was finally able to leave her teaching position and write full time. Other novels followed, including a book intended as a primer for elementary school students titled, "The Wonderful Adventures of Nils."

Christmas in Bethlehem. The ancient dream:
a cold, clear night made brilliant by a glorious star,
the smell of incense, shepherds
and wise men falling to their knees in adoration
of the sweet baby, the incarnation of perfect love.

LUCINDA FRANKS

Away in a Manger

Author Unknown

Away in a manger, no crib for a bed,
The little Lord Jesus laid down His sweet head.
The stars in the sky looked down where He lay,
The little Lord Jesus asleep on the hay.

The cattle are lowing, the baby awakes,
But little Lord Jesus no crying He makes.
I love Thee, Lord Jesus, look down from the sky
And stay by my cradle 'til morning is nigh.

Be near me, Lord Jesus, I ask Thee to stay,
Close by me forever, and love me, I pray.
Bless all the dear children in Thy tender care,
And take us to heaven, to live with Thee there.

HISTORICAL NOTE:

Many have the misconception that Martin Luther wrote this sweet Christmas carol, but historians say the first two verses were originally published in a Lutheran Sunday school book in 1885, author unknown. Its title in the song book, "Luther's Cradle Hymn," is probably the source of the confusion. Some credit the music to James R. Murray, while others believe he merely harmonized an old German folk song. The words are frequently sung to the tune of the Scottish song "Flow Gently Sweet Afton."

OUT OF THE MOUTHS OF BABES

FROM THE JOYFUL NZ NEWSLETTER

When a pastor asked the class, "Why was Jesus born in Bethlehem?" A boy raised his hand and replied, "Because his mother was there."

REV. WILLIAM ARMSTRONG, S.J.

A Sunday school teacher asked her class why Joseph and Mary took Jesus with them to Jerusalem. "They couldn't get a baby-sitter," a small child replied.

VIA CATHERINE HALL, PITTSBURGH, PA

A Sunday school teacher was telling her class of fourth-graders the Christmas story of three Wise Men bringing gifts to the Baby Jesus.

A little girl who had recently become the big sister of a brand-new brother said: "Well, I guess gold and all that stuff are all right, but I'll bet Mary really wished somebody had brought some diapers."

VIA JIM MCDONOUGH, STONE MOUNTAIN, GA

"One of the members of our church invited his brother and his family to our Christmas service. During the service, the four-year-old boy began squirming in the pew and whispered to his daddy that he had to go to the potty.

"The father took the boy's hand and escorted him up the aisle to the rest room. About halfway down the aisle, the little guy, stopped, turned around, and said loud and clear: 'I have to go potty, God, but I'll be right back!'"

MRS. MARJORIE DIGGINS, MARSHALLTOWN, IA

A mother discovered her five-year-old daughter drawing with her crayons on some paper. "What are you drawing?" she asked.

"A picture of God," the little girl said.

The mother replied: "No one knows what God looks like."

"They will when I get through," the girl said.

Via Catherine Hall, Pittsburgh, PA[9]

Did You Know?

At midnight on Christmas Eve, 1914, firing from the German trenches suddenly stopped. A German brass band began playing Christmas carols. Early Christmas morning, the German soldiers came out of their trenches, approaching the allied lines, calling "Merry Christmas." At first the allied soldiers thought it was a trick, but they soon climbed out of their trenches and shook hands with the German soldiers. The truce lasted a few days, and the men exchanged presents of cigarettes and plum puddings and sang carols and songs.

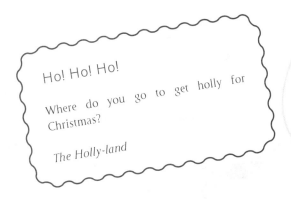

Ho! Ho! Ho!

Where do you go to get holly for Christmas?

The Holly-land

Pavlova

3 egg whites

1 pinch of salt

$^3/_4$ cup castor sugar

$^1/_4$ cup white sugar

1 Tbsp. corn flour

1 tsp. lemon juice

$^1/_2$ pint cream

Kiwi fruit or strawberries for garnish

Preheat the oven to 300°F (The temperature is reduced for baking.)

Beat the egg whites to a foam. Add the salt and beat until the mixture forms soft peaks which fold over when the beater is removed. Slowly beat in the castor sugar, beating well after each addition. Keep beating until the mixture is stiff and the peaks stand up when the beater is removed. Mix together the white sugar and corn flour. Lightly fold into the meringue with the lemon juice.

Line an oven tray with baking paper. Spread the meringue into a circle and pipe a decoration around the edge or swirl with a spoon if desired. Bake in a cool oven (180°F) for 2 to 2 $^1/_2$ hours. Turn off the heat and leave in the oven overnight to cool.

Top with whipped cream and decorate with sliced kiwi-fruit, sliced strawberries, passion fruit, or just about any tropical fruit, just before serving.

GINGERBREAD MEN

3 1/4 cups all-purpose flour

1/4 tsp. salt

1/2 tsp. baking soda

1/4 tsp. ground cloves

2 tsp. ground ginger

1 tsp. ground cinnamon

2 sticks butter, softened to room temperature

3/4 cup firmly packed dark brown sugar

1 large egg

1/2 cup unsulphured molasses

2/3 cup confectioners' sugar

1 to 2 tsp. milk

Whisk together first 6 ingredients. Set aside. In separate bowl, cream butter and sugar with a mixer. Add egg and molasses; beat on medium until mixture is smooth. Add the flour mixture a little at a time. Blend on low just until mixture is combined. Divide dough in half and form into flat rounds. Cover each tightly with plastic wrap. Chill for 1 hour or until firm.

Preheat oven to 325°F.

Flour rolling pin and board. Roll each half of dough out to form a 1/4-inch thickness. Flour cookie cutters; cut out gingerbread people. Continue to roll and cut out dough until all is used. Place 1/2 inch apart on ungreased cookie sheets. Bake for 9 to 11 minutes. Do not brown. Use a spatula to place on flat surface to cool.

Combine confectioners' sugar and milk in a small bowl. Stir until smooth. If too dry, add more milk a bit at a time. Place icing in a pastry bag with a small tip. Decorate cookies. Makes about 40 cookies.

CHRISTMAS FRUITCAKE

History: The earliest fruitcake recipe in existence came from ancient Rome and was made of pomegranate seeds, pine nuts, and raisins mixed into barley mash. In the Middle Ages, honey, spices, and preserved fruits were added, and the name *fruitcake* was first used.

In the U.S. the fruitcake has become one of the most ridiculed desserts and the butt of many jokes centered on its heaviness and long shelf life. Former *Tonight Show* host Johnny Carson joked that there really is only one fruitcake in the world. It is passed from family to family—a joke also frequently attributed to the writer Calvin Trillin, who denies being the source.

For many years, Manitou Springs, Colorado, has hosted the Great Fruitcake Toss. Recycled fruitcakes are recommended by event planners. The all-time Great Fruitcake Toss record is 420 feet.

Fruitcakes have been banned on airplanes. Due to their density, it is possible for a weapon to be baked inside the cake to avoid detection.

Generally, fruitcake is a mixture of fruits and nuts with just enough batter to hold them together. When wrapped in cheesecloth and foil, saturated with alcoholic liquors regularly, and kept in tightly closed tins, a fruitcake may be kept for months or even years. The recipe itself takes only about two hours and a basic understanding of the kitchen to master. You will need to begin in October or early November, however, in order for the cake to be ready by Christmastime.

In the UK, fruitcakes are far moister and richer than their American counterparts, and remain extremely popular. The traditional Christmas cake is a fruitcake covered in marzipan, and then in white satin or royal icing. They are often further decorated with snow scenes, holly leaves and berries (real or artificial), or tiny decorative robins or snowmen.

Despite its detractors, a rich homemade fruitcake is incredibly delicious and has all the makings of being the star of the Christmas dinner. Made out of the best fresh fruits, nuts, and complex spices, it definitely adds an elegant touch of tradition to Christmas celebrations.

Top Ten Favorite Christmas Toys of All Time for Girls

1. Barbie and Ken dolls
2. Roller or ice skates
3. Stuffed animals
4. Crayons
5. Jump rope
6. Jacks
7. Easy-Bake Oven
8. Pinwheels
9. Candy Land board game
10. Books

Christmas is based on an exchange of gifts:
the gift of God to man—
his Son; and the gift of man to God—
when we first give ourselves to God.

VANCE HAVNER

December 20

From home to home and heart to heart,
from one place to another.
The warmth and joy of Christmas brings us
closer to each other.

AUTHOR UNKNOWN

CHRISTMAS IN THE HEART

RACHEL FIELD

*Y*ears ago two little girls trudged up a long hill in the twilight of late December. They carried a basket between them, and one was I, and one was Helga Swanson. The smell of warm coffeecake and braided cinnamon bread and little brown twists like deer horns comes back to me now from that remembered basket. Sweeter than all the perfumes of Arabia that fragrance reached our half-frozen noses, yet we never lifted the folded napkin, for we took our responsibility hard. Helga's mother and grandmother had spent the better part of three days over that Christmas baking, and we had been chosen to deliver it and help trim the tree at the Lutheran Home on the hill above the Fallen Leaf Lake.

"We must hurry," Helga said. "They've lighted the parlors already."

I could hardly see Helga's face for the darkness, but I felt her warm, vigorous presence beside me in her tightly buttoned coat and knitted tam that half covered her fair braids. I would be seven in another month, and she had been eight last March when we had moved from the state of Maine to Minnesota. It had seemed strange and a little frightening to me then to hear so many people speaking to one another in words I couldn't understand. Helga, herself, could drop into Swedish if it seemed worth her while to join in such conversations.

"It's nothing. I'll teach you," she had promised. But her enthusiasm had waned after a few attempts. So Helga became my interpreter as well as my most intimate friend. Without her I should never have known the old men and women in the red brick house who were our hosts that night. I should never have seen Pastor Hanson bending over the melodeon or heard old Christine Berglund tell about the star.

"Merry Christmas!" we called even before the door was thrown open and the spiciness of cooking food came out to us as from the gates of heaven.

There were sixteen of us, counting Helga and me, round that table with its white cloth, and its soup tureen at one end and round yellow cheese at the other. We all stood at our places while Pastor Hanson said a blessing in Swedish.

"There is a church in every man's heart," I remember, he said in English at the end of his prayer, "but let us be sure that it is always God who preaches the sermon."

The smell from those bowls of pea soup stays with me yet! Golden and smooth and rich to the last spoonful, we ate it with slices of fresh rye bread and home-churned butter. Pastor Hanson, himself, sliced the cheese with a knife that shaved it into one yellow curl after another. Cinnamon and coffee and hot bread and molasses mingled in one delicious scent as dishes and cups and plates passed from hand to hand.

At last we gathered in the parlor and another scuttle of coal went into the big stove. The time had come for decorating the tree, and everyone took a hand in it except old Mrs. Berglund, who stayed in a wheel chair because of her rheumatism. But even she gave advice about where more strings of popcorn were needed and if the candles were placed where they would show best among the green branches. Mr. Johnson had made birds out of pine cones, and there were cranberries in long strings as red as the popcorn was white. There were hearts and crescents of tinfoil and balls made out of bright bits of worsted. But there was no star anywhere, and I wondered about that; for no Christmas tree could be complete without a star to light its tip. But I need not have been troubled about that, as it turned out.

Pastor Hanson went over to the melodeon against the wall and began to play a Christmas carol. When we had finished, someone went over and whispered to old Mrs. Berglund in her wheel chair. From under the shawl she took out a small box that she held fast in her hands, which were thin and crooked as apple twigs. It was very still in the room for a moment, the kind of stillness that makes you know something exceedingly important is going to happen.

"Well, Pastor Hanson," she said, and held out the little box, "I did not think God would spare me for another year, but here I am, and here is the Christmas star."

"You must tell the children," he said. "It is right that they should hear before we hang it on the tree."

"Yust like tonight it vas," Christine Berglund began, and I felt grateful that she was telling it so for my sake, even though her j's and y's and v's and w's had a way of changing places as she said them, "I vere eleven year old then and sick in my heart because Christmas is coming and I am so far from my mother and brothers and sisters—"

I could see that big country estate as she told us about it—the stone walls and courtyard, the park with its thick woods; the tiled floors and great fireplaces; the heavy, carved furniture, the enormous beds that would have held her whole family of brothers and sisters. She was young to be sent away into service, and everything and everyone in that house was old, from the mistress to the servants who had tended her for many years.

Pastor Lange came once each month to hold service in the stone chapel, because his parish church was too far away for the servants to attend. Pastor Lange was a very kind old man, and Christine did not feel so lonely on the days when he came. He always spent the night there and, though the mistress of the house never went into the chapel, after the service was over she sent for him and they ate supper together and talked before the fire until bedtime. Christine knew this because once she was sent with a tray from the kitchen to set before them.

"God bless you, my child," Pastor Lange had said. "May you rest well."

But the old lady had kept her lips shut in a thin line, and she would not let her eyes rest on her young serving maid. It was the next morning that Pastor Lange answered Christine's questions. Their mistress had hardened her heart against every living thing because years ago she had lost her only child, a daughter as good as she was gay and beautiful. When death had taken her child the mother had turned as cold and gray as a boulder. She had ordered the girl's room closed and the birds let out of their cages. She had had a cloth hung over her portrait and every reminder of her presence taken from each nook and corner. Worst of all, she had summoned Pastor Lange and told him that she would live if she must, but he need never look for her in the family pew again. God had forsaken her, and Sunday and Easter and Christmas would be for her as any other days.

And she had kept her vow, though Pastor Lange had never ceased to pray that a miracle might turn her bitterness into faith once more.

"And did it?" Helga and I interrupted in our impatience.

But the story could not be hurried.

"Christmas it is the vorst," old Christine went on, "for in that big house there is not one cake baked or one bit of green hung on any door. At home ve are poor, but ve put out grain for the birds and have our candles to light and our songs to sing."

Each night she cried as the holiday grew near. She thought of her mother and brothers and sisters all together in a house that was small but savory with holiday cooking. She thought also of the little church on Christmas Eve, with its lighted windows, and the graves outside, each with a torch set there to burn through the long hours till Christmas morning. It was right, her mother had told her, that even the dead should join with the living on that Holy Night. And there was nothing that Christine could do, a half-grown girl in that house of silence and old, old people, to show that Christmas was in her heart.

But once she had noticed near the chapel some tilted gravestones and among them one not so cold and gray as the others. Lichens covered the letters cut upon it. She was afraid to scrape away the moss to read the name, but there could be no harm, she thought, in putting a branch of green upon it. Perhaps she might even take her own candle out there to burn and say a prayer and sing a carol. The thought of that made her feel less lonely. She hummed a Christmas hymn as she went back to her work, and it was as she crossed the courtyard that something bright caught her eye in a crack between two flagstones. She bent to pick it up and there, half hidden by moss, was a pin, star-shaped and shining and giving out jets of color as she turned it in the sun.

"Like the Star of Bethlehem," she thought, and her heart beat fast under the apron she wore, for surely it seemed like a sign to comfort her.

She pinned it where no one would see it under her dress, and all day she felt it close to her heart as she went about her duties. That night she slept with it beneath her pillow, and she thought of the Wise Men of old who had seen that other star in the East and followed it to Bethlehem.

Next day she slipped out and stopped by the gravestones. On the smallest stone she set a green branch of fir with cones. It stood straight and fine— almost, Christine Berglund told us, like the Christmas tree we had just trimmed.

"That night is Christmas Eve," she went on, "and I think there can be no harm if I go out after it is dark and light my candle and set the star there to keep watch till it is morning."

But, as the afternoon passed and twilight came, Christine did not feel so happy. The hidden star pricked her with its points, almost as if it were her own conscience telling her that stars were not meant to be hidden, that what we pick up is not ours merely for the finding. She tried to tell herself that it would be different if she had found her treasure in the house, not out there between the stones of the courtyard.

So darkness fell, and it was Christmas Eve. Some of the old servants remembered and spoke of other times when there had been laughter and festivity in those rooms, and the chapel bell ringing to call them to midnight service. Christine sat quiet until she could slip away to her little room. It was chill there in the darkness because she dared not waste her candle.

At last the fires were banked and the house grew silent. Then Christine put on her cloak and crept down the stairs. She let herself into the courtyard, where nothing stirred but the shadows of trees beyond the walls. The moon was high above the stone turrets. She and it seemed to be the only things which moved in that world of winter quiet. She passed the chapel where no bells pealed from the dark belfry. There were the old tilted gravestones and the one with the bit of green to mark it. Her fingers shook as she set her candle on the headstone and tried to light it. Twice it went out before the small flame shone clear. Her hands still trembled as she took out the star and pinned it among the green needles.

"And then I get down on my knees and first I say 'Our Father.' Then I make another one that is mine, so God shall know that I do not forget the night of our Saviour's birth. It is hard for me to find the words for my prayer and my teeth are chattering like little hammers, so I don't hear someone come tap-tapping on the stones—"

"Oh!" Helga and I drew sharp breaths. "Who was it?"

But old Christine must tell the story her own way.

"There I am on my knees," she repeated, "praying to God, and my candle is still burning. Yes, that is how she found me."

We dared not interrupt her again, but our eyes never left her face.

"'Mistress, I said," she went on, "'forgive me.' But she don't answer me; she yust stand there and turn it in her hands, and she act like she is seeing a ghost."

They must have stood so a long time. The candle burned out on the headstone before the old mistress took Christine back to the house. She did not speak until they reached the great hall, though tears ran down her cheeks at each step they took. Her hands reached for the bell rope, and the house echoed to her frantic ringing. Christine could hear the servants hurrying to and fro upstairs in answer to the summons.

"I think she send for them because I have done a bad thing," old Christine told us, "so I stand and shiver there and don't know what is going to happen to me. And then they come down, all so sleepy they forget to make their curtsies. And Mistress point to me, and I cry so I don't see her face anymore. But she say to them, 'Go; make a fire in the blocker room. Spread linen and blankets on the bed and warm it, and bring food, that this child may eat and be comforted.' I think I don't hear her right, but they take me there, and I see the fire lighted and the bed vaiting, so I don't try to think anymore. I yust lie down with flowers spread over me, and I sleep and sleep. And there is no one to come and shake me at sunrise to help in the kitchen. I vake, and it is Christmas morning and bells are ringing so sweet I think I dream them from home. But they are ringing in the chapel. Then the maids come and bring me a beautiful dress that smells of cloves and lavender. And they dress me in it, and I ask them the meaning of all this; but they yust smile and say, 'Pastor Lange, he vill tell you.'"

And, sure enough, Pastor Lange and the old mistress came from the chapel. He had driven since sunrise in the carriage she had sent to bring him there.

"You shall see for yourself, Pastor," the old coachman had said, "that the day of miracles is not past."

So Christine went down to meet them in the dress that was heavy with gold embroidery and slippers so soft she seemed to be walking on snow. These rooms were no longer gray and gloomy but warm with leaping fires. The covers were gone from the portrait of a laughing girl no older than she. Her dress

253

was the same that Christine wore, and the star showed plainly on the painted folds. Christine marveled at each change she saw about her, most of all at her mistress's face, which was still sad, but no longer set like stone.

Then Pastor Lange put his hands on Christine's head and blessed her in God's name. But to the old woman he said, "Blessed are they that mourn, for they shall be comforted."

And Christine sat between them at dinner, and felt strange that she should now be served who had so lately carried in the dishes.

"And after dinner is over Pastor Lange he tells me that it is indeed a miracle God has worked through me to bring faith to our mistress. I don't understand how that can be, for it was not right that I keep the pin and tell no one. But Pastor Lange does not know how to explain that to me. So he says, 'Christine, it must have been that God vas in your heart to do this thing.' 'No, Pastor,' I tell him the truth; 'it was Christmas in my heart.' And Pastor Lange he don't scold me, he yust say maybe that is the same thing."

Old Christine was growing tired. Her voice had dwindled to a thin thread of sound by the time she had answered our questions … Yes, the pin had belonged to her mistress's daughter. She had lost it one winter day and grown so chill hunting for it in the courtyard that she had fallen ill and died. It was her gravestone by the chapel that Christine had chosen to light and decorate with green. So great had been that mother's grief that it was more than thirty years since she had spoken her daughter's name or let anything be a reminder. But Christine's candle shining on Christmas Eve had been like a sign sent from her dead child by a living one on that most happy night of the year.

So Christine no longer served as a maid in that great house. She lived as the old woman's daughter, and in winter the rooms were warm and bright with fires and laughter, and in summer sweet with flowers and the singing of birds.

"And see, here is the star to hang on the tree."

"The same one? The very same?"

"Yes, the same. It goes with me always since that night."

We touched the five shining points with wonder in our finger tips before Christine's old fingers lifted it from the bed of cotton.

"Real diamonds and not one missing," she said proudly as she handed it to Captain Christiansen, because he was tall enough to set it on the topmost tip.

"But I never think it vould come all the vay to America. I never think I come all that vay myself."

We watched it send out little jets of brightness when the candles were lighted below and all the old faces shining in the loveliest of light. We sang another carol all together, and then it was time to go home with Helga's father, who had come for us.

"Good night." Their voices followed us to the door. "God Jul! Merry Christmas!"

"Merry Christmas!" Helga and I called back before we turned to follow her father's lantern into the wintry dark. ✳

RACHEL FIELD (1894–1942)

This wonderful American author is best known for her children's books. She won a Newbery Medal in 1930 for her book *Hitty, Her First Hundred Years* (1929). While in a shop in New York City, Field and the book's illustrator came across an antique doll that later inspired Hitty's doll adventures. Field has also written a children's novel about pioneer life titled *Calico Bush* (1931), several books of poetry, and several plays for children. Her writing also includes novels for adult readers.

Sugar Cutout Cookies

1 cup (2 sticks) butter, softened

1 cup sugar

2 eggs, well beaten

2 tsp. vanilla extract

3 1/2 cups sifted all-purpose flour

2 tsp. baking powder

Preheat the oven to 375°F.

Combine butter, sugar, beaten eggs, and vanilla in a large mixer bowl. Cream with electric mixer until fluffy. Resift flour with baking powder and blend with other ingredients at low speed, slowly and gradually, until well mixed. Chill dough thoroughly.

Tear off one-quarter to one-third of the dough, form into a ball, and roll out on lightly floured wax paper until approximately 1/4-inch thick. Cut out Christmas shapes with floured cookie cutters. Decorate cookies before baking with color sugar crystals, nonpareils, silver balls, and the like—or after baking with icing described below. Place on greased cookie sheet and bake for 10 to 15 minutes or until golden. Remove and cool on a wire rack. Repeat with rest of the dough.

Makes about 4 dozen, depending upon size of cutters.

ICING FOR DECORATED COOKIES

     3 egg whites

     1 tsp. cream of tartar

     1 16-ounce box confectioners' sugar

     Food coloring

Beat together egg whites, cream of tartar, and confectioners' sugar. Mix in food coloring. Spread icing on cookies with a knife or decorate cookie using a pastry tube.

A BIRTHDAY PARTY

EILEEN KEY

*A*s Christmas approached, I found myself cloaked in sadness; the thought of trimming the tree and buying gifts only depressed me more. I was a single mother with three children who needed to capture the magic of the season, yet for me, there was no magic. Since my divorce, I'd seen only financial hardship, loneliness, and grief. I wanted to bypass the season completely.

My plastic smile and hollow greetings during the holidays only made my empty heart lonelier. Struggling with the checkbook, I managed to shuffle bills and allow a small budget for gifts. My heart in my throat, I watched each cash register total and applied mental math skills to work around a shrinking budget. Using colorful comic pages for wrapping paper economized more. Gifts given to me at work became gifts to others, saving yet another expense.

Christmas Day loomed. A feast prepared for the four of us? No extra chair at the table? Loneliness clouded my mind. The words of my children blew away the fog.

"Mom, may we make a birthday cake for Jesus this year?"

Jesus' birthday?

Of course, the celebration was for the baby Jesus. In my despair, I'd forgotten to focus on the true "reason for the season." We were celebrating the birthday of the Christ child. The holiday was not just gift giving to others, parties for couples, and blinking lights once strung by husbands. The holiday was a reminder of the precious gift given to us by the Father. The gift of Jesus.

My focus shifted. I loved birthday parties. Mentally changing the former holiday traditions to a birthday party for Jesus turned my depression into joy. Giving to others became a pleasure again.

The children and I decorated our home, eager to make it special. We had a Guest coming. The tree lights shone on our faces when we flipped the switch. Each point of color warmed me inside. I knew our joyful smiles pleased Him.

Time slipped by as we readied for the day. On Christmas Eve, we baked a luscious two layer cake, topped with butter-cream frosting and a bright red candle. We gathered around the table to a simple meal and brought out the dessert. We sang "Happy Birthday" to Jesus, and together blew out the candle. We saved the joy of opening our gifts for the morning, choosing instead to visit our neighbors and share our cake.

We spread the word: We'd had a birthday party at our house! ✶

Blessed be God for His unspeakable gift, we need Him.
Souls desire Him as the heart panteth after the water brooks.
He came to the world in the fullness of time. He comes at this Advent
season to us. Today may be for some soul here the fullness of time.
Let us open the gates and admit Him, that this Christ may be our
Christ forever; that living with Him and dying with Him,
we may also be glorified together with Him.

DAVID JAMES BURRELL

December 21

HERE IS LOVE
JOHN BUNYAN

Here is love, that God
Sent His Son,
His Son who never offended,
His Son who was always
His delight.

TWINKLE

HAROLD LEONARD BOWMAN

*T*winkle was a mischievous little angel who loved to play in the streets of heaven. There were many happy cherubs there, but Twinkle had a bubbling boyishness, which made him popular with his friends. There was a glint of playfulness in his eyes which won him his name. He was known occasionally to play tricks that disturbed some of the older and more sedate angels. Sometimes at a serious moment, he would lift his eyes and wink at some sober, elderly angel who, in spite of himself, could not help smiling back at the little fellow with his downy wings. Twinkle had a lovely little silver halo which he usually wore tiled a bit to one side—as no proper angel should.

One day word went around heaven that a great event was to occur on a distant star called "the earth" and that a company of angels was going on a journey to celebrate this important occasion. Twinkle did not understand what it was all about, but when a crowd gathered he was always there. So now Twinkle tagged along.

The angels flew rapidly to the earth and delivered their message, announcing the birth of a child who was to be a Savior, a Lord of Goodwill, a Prince of Peace. As the angelic chorus sang, little Twinkle fluttered about on the edge of the cherubic host.

Their mission performed, the angels started back to heaven. But Twinkle was a curious little fellow, and he wanted to see what this was about which the angels were so excited. So he decided to find out. Instead of returning with his friend, he settled down to the dark hillside and, keeping well in the shadows, he followed the shepherds who were going to investigate the news the angels had brought.

Twinkle saw the shepherds go into a nearby town and then into a stable. A little frightened by these dark and unfamiliar surroundings, Twinkle kept out of sight until the shepherds emerged and returned to their flocks on the hillsides.

Then very quietly Twinkle tiptoed over to the door of the stable, gently pushed it open and stepped inside without a sound. At first he was puzzled. What was so wonderful about this? Just a woman holding something in her arms. She looked up and saw this chubby little angel standing there. Partly through embarrassment and partly because he was the kind of angel he was, Twinkle winked at the woman. She smiled—a gracious, gentle smile it was, that encouraged him; so he came closer and then he saw the little baby in her arms—the most beautiful little babe that Twinkle had ever seen, so helpless but so dear. So this was to be a Savior; this infant was one whose advent heaven was celebrating. The twinkle in the little angel's eyes brightened. He reached up to his silver halo—it was tilted on the side, as usual—and took it off and, reaching it out, placed it on the head of the babe. Again the child's mother smiled, in gratitude. She reached out her hand to touch Twinkle, but he, started by his daring, turned and fled into the night.

He was out of breath and his wings were worn when he finally reached the gates of heaven.

Hearing his clamor for admission, St. Peter opened the portal and greeted him with a stern reproof. "Twinkle, where have you been? And what have you done with your halo? Have you got into trouble again?" Twinkle slipped in without answering. But the story soon spread and everyone wondered how Twinkle had lost his lovely silver halo. Such misbehavior as this must be brought to the attention on the Father who ruled in heaven. So when all the celestial company was gathered about the great white throne, little Twinkle came and stood alone amid the reproachful looks of the other angels.

"Father," he said, "forgive me for losing my halo. I gave it to the little babe in the manger in Bethlehem." A murmur of disapproval swept through the host of angels—that one of their number should think so little of his halo as to give it away.

But the Father looked at Twinkle and smiled. "You have done well," he said. And then the angels who were watching Twinkle were amazed to see shining above his face a new halo, brighter than the other, for this one was of purest gold. Twinkle felt it on his head; he reached up to touch it with his hand, to make sure it was real; it was. He gave it a slight tilt to one side—for that was the jaunty sort of angel Twinkle was. ✳

THE SHEPHERD SPEAKS

JOHN ERSKINE

Out of the midnight sky a great dawn broke,
And a voice singing flooded us with song.
In David's city was He born, it sang.
A Saviour, Christ the Lord. Then while I sat
Shivering with the thrill of that great cry,
A mighty choir a thousandfold more sweet
Suddenly sang, Glory to God, and Peace—
Peace on the earth; my heart, almost unnerved
By the swift loveliness, would hardly beat.
Speechless we waited till the accustomed night
Gave us no promise more sweet surprise;
Then scrambling to our feet, without a word
We started through the fields to find the Child.

CHRISTMAS DINNER IN ITALY

Traditional Italian Menu
Christmas Eve:
Broccoli rabe (also known as Christmas broccoli)
Vermicelli with anchovies or clams
Large eel, roasted, baked, or fried
Additional fish dishes from baccalà to baked fish to lobster.
Caponata di pesce (fish salad)
Seafood stew
Shrimp and orange salad
Dried fruit
Desserts: paste reali, susamielli, rococo, and mustacciuoli with nut crunch

Christmas Day:
Baked pasta (lasagna or timpano)
Roasted fish, turkey, capanata
Struffoli (honey balls)
Panettone (bread made with raisins and candied fruit)
Pandoro (airy, buttery Christmas cake from Verona)
Panforte (variation on pound cake made with almonds, honey, flour, and candied fruit)

The History
- The Christmas season in Italy goes for three weeks. Known as the Novena, it begins eight days before Christmas.
- During Novena, children go from house to house reciting Christmas poems and singing.

- In the week before Christmas, children go from house to house dressed as shepherds, playing pipes, singing, and reciting Christmas poems. They are given money to buy presents.
- Presents and empty boxes are drawn from the Urn of Fate, which always contains one gift per person. At twilight, candles are lighted around the family crib known as the precipio, prayers are said, and children recite poems.
- A strict meat fast is observed for twenty-four hours before Christmas Eve, ending with a meatless celebration meal called cenone, which can consist of as many as twenty courses.
- A Christmas lunch is prepared for Christmas Day and another dinner (prima festa) is served on the day after Christmas.
- Tortellini or ravioli is usually the fare for prima festa.

Did You Know?

- All Christmas sweets contain nuts and almonds. Folklore theorizes that to eat nuts favors the fertility of the earth and aids in the increase of flocks and family.
- In Italy, children wait until Epiphany on January 6 to open their gifts.

For Our Italian Friends: Buon Natale! This traditional Christmas greeting actually means "Good birthday."

Christmas Wassail

1 gallon apple cider (strain out the apple bits)
1 tsp. ground cloves
1 tsp. ground allspice
1 tsp. ground nutmeg
1 tsp. ground cinnamon
1 6-ounce can frozen lemonade, thawed
1 6-ounce can frozen orange juice, thawed
$1/2$ cup firmly packed brown sugar

Combine 2 cups apple cider and spices in a large pan; bring to a boil. Reduce heat and simmer for 10 minutes. Add remaining cider and other ingredients and heat until hot. Do not boil.

BALLAD FOR CHRISTMAS

NANCY BYRD TURNER

It's time to welcome Christmas, now.
Off to the woods for wintry vine,
For white and scarlet-berried bough
And patterned fir and frosty pine,
For logs to make the broad hearth shine—
Stout oak, and hickory, dry and hale,
To send a glow across the snow!
The light of Christmas shall not fail.
Under the old and arching skies
Clear carols call, by street and hill;
The stars that saw the great Star rise
Are shining still, are shining still.
In all the long years, come what will,
There's nothing new and nothing strange
In one old night of song and light—
The heart of Christmas cannot change!

*There are three stages of man: he believes in Santa Claus,
he doesn't believe in Santa Claus, he is Santa Claus.*

BOB PHILLIPS

FRANKINCENSE AND MYRRH

HEYWOOD BROUN

*O*nce there were three kings in the East and they were wise men. They read the heavens and they saw a certain strange star by which they knew that in a distant land the King of the World was to be born. The star beckoned to them and they made preparations for a long journey.

From their palaces they gathered rich gifts, gold and frankincense and myrrh. Great sacks of precious stuffs were loaded upon the backs of the camels which were to bear them on their journey. Everything was in readiness, but one of the wise men seemed perplexed and would not come at once to join his two companions, who were eager and impatient to be on their way in the direction indicated by the star.

They were old, these two kings, and the other wise man was young. When they asked him, he could not tell why he waited. He knew that his treasures had been ransacked for rich gifts for the King of Kings. It seemed that there was nothing more which he could give, and yet he was not content.

He made no answer to the old men who shouted to him that the time had come. The camels were impatient and swayed and snarled. The shadows across the desert grew longer. And still the young king sat and thought deeply.

At length he smiled, and he ordered his servants to open the great treasure sack upon the back of the first of his camels. Then he went into a high chamber to which he had not been since he was a child. He rummaged about and presently came out and approached the caravan. In his hand he carried something which glinted in the sun.

The kings thought that he bore some new gift more rare and precious than any which they had been able to find in all their treasure rooms. They bent down to see, and even the camel drivers peered from the backs of the great beasts to find out what it was which gleamed in the sun. They were curious about the last gift for which all the caravan had waited.

And the young king took a toy from his hand and placed it upon the sand. It was a dog of tin, painted white and speckled with black spots. Great patches of paint had worn away and left the metal clear, and that was why the toy shone in the sun as if it had been silver.

The youngest of the wise men turned a key in the side of the little black and white dog and then he stepped aside so that the kings and the camel drivers could see. The dog leaped high in the air and turned a somersault. He turned another and another and then fell over upon his side and lay there with a set and painted grin upon his face.

A child, the son of a camel driver, laughed and clapped his hands, but the kings were stern. They rebuked the youngest of the wise men and he paid no attention but called to his chief servant to make the first of all the camels kneel. Then he picked up the toy of tin and, opening the treasure sack, placed his last gift with his own hands in the mouth of the sack so that it rested safely upon the soft bags of incense.

"What folly has seized you?" cried the eldest of the wise men. "Is this a gift to bear to the King of Kings in the far country?"

And the young man answered and said: "For the King of Kings here are gifts of great richness, gold and frankincense and myrrh. "But this, he said, "is for the child in Bethlehem." ✳

As many mince pies as you taste at Christmas,
so many happy months will you have.

OLD ENGLISH SAYING

WE WISH YOU A MERRY CHRISTMAS

TRADITIONAL ENGLISH CAROL

We wish you a merry Christmas
We wish you a merry Christmas
We wish you a merry Christmas
And a happy New Year.
Glad tidings we bring
To you and your kin;
Glad tidings for Christmas
And a happy New Year!

We want some figgy pudding
We want some figgy pudding
We want some figgy pudding
Please bring it right here!
Glad tidings we bring
To you and your kin;
Glad tidings for Christmas
And a happy New Year!

We won't go until we get some
We won't go until we get some
We won't go until we get some
So bring it out here!
Glad tidings we bring
To you and your kin;

Glad tidings for Christmas
And a happy New Year!

We wish you a Merry Christmas
We wish you a Merry Christmas
We wish you a Merry Christmas
And a happy New Year.
Glad tidings we bring
To you and your kin;
Glad tidings for Christmas
And a happy New Year!

HISTORICAL NOTE:

Music played a major role in early England because it was essentially the only form of entertainment available. Bands of singers pitched products for sale, greeted visiting dignitaries, and played at weddings. Waits—as the singers were called—were especially busy at Christmastime. Bands of singers could be seen everywhere standing in the snow, telling the story of the nativity in song, and adding to the festivities. They usually received a coin, a bit of fig pudding, spiced ale, or some roasted pig in return. Many of the oldest and most popular Christmas carols, including this one, have been attributed to the Waits.

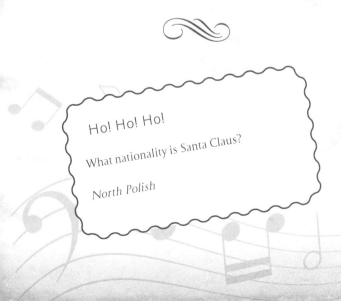

Ho! Ho! Ho!

What nationality is Santa Claus?

North Polish

December 22

*The message of Christmas is
that the visible material world is
bound to the invisible spiritual world.*

AUTHOR UNKNOWN

The Angel and the Shepherds

Lew Wallace

A mile and a half, it may be two miles, southeast of Bethlehem there is a plain separated from the town by an intervening swell of the mountain—

At the side farthest from the town, and close under a bluff, there was an extensive *marah*, or sheep-cote, ages old. In some long-forgotten foray the building had been unroofed and almost demolished. The enclosure attached to it remained in tact, however, and that was of more importance to the shepherds who drove their charges thither than the house itself—

There were six of these men, omitting the watchman, and after a while they assembled in a group near the fire, some sitting and some lying prone—

They rested and talked; and their talk was all about their flocks, a dull theme to the world, and yet a theme which was all the world to them—

While they talked, and before the first watch was over, one by one the shepherds went to sleep, each lying where he had sat.

The night, like most nights of the winter season in the hill country, was clear, crisp, and sparkling with stars. There was no wind. The atmosphere seemed never so pure, the stillness was more than silence; it was a holy hush, a warning that heaven was stooping low to whisper some good thing to the listening earth.

By the gate, hugging his mantle close, the watchman walked; at times he stopped, attracted by a stir among the sleeping herd, or by a jackal's cry off on the mountainside. The midnight was slow in coming to him, but at last it came. His task was done; and now for the dreamless sleep with which labor blesses its wearied children! He moved toward the fire, but paused; a light was breaking around him, soft and white, like the moon's. He waited breathlessly. The light deepened; things before invisible came into view; he saw the whole field, and all it sheltered. A chill sharper than that of the frosty air—a chill of fear—smote him. He looked up; the stars were gone; the light was dropping as from a window in the sky; and as he looked it became a splendor; then, in terror, he cried, "Awake, awake!"

Up he sprang and the dogs, howling, ran away.

The herds rushed together, bewildered.

The men clambered to their feet, weapons in hand.

"What is it?" they asked in one voice.

"See!" cried the watchman, "the sky is on fire!"

Suddenly the light became intolerably bright, and they covered their eyes and dropped upon their knees; then as their souls shrank with fear, they fell upon their faces, blind and fainting, and would have died had not a voice said unto them: "Fear not!"

And they listened.

"Fear not; for behold, I bring you good tidings of great joy, which shall be to all people. For unto you, this day, in the city of David, is born a Saviour, which is Christ the Lord! And this shall be a sign unto you, ye shall find the babe wrapped in swaddling clothes and lying in a manger."

The voice in sweetness and soothing more than human, and low and clear, penetrated all their being and filled them with assurance. They rose upon their knees, and looking worshipfully up, beheld in the center of a great glory the appearance of a man, clad in a robe intensely white; above its shoulders towered the stops of wings shining and folded. A star over its forehead glowed with a steady luster, brilliant as Hesperus. Its hands were stretched toward them in blessing; its face was serene and divinely beautiful.

The herald spoke not again; his good tidings were told; and yet he stayed awhile. Then suddenly the light, of which he seemed the center, turned roseate and began to tremble; and then up, as far as the men could see, there was a flashing of white wings, and a coming and going of radiant forms, and voices as of a whole multitude chanting in unison, "Glory to God in the highest, and on earth, peace, goodwill to men!"

Then the shepherds said one to another, "Come let us take a wee ewe lamb from the fold, and go yonder to Bethlehem, and see this thing which has come to pass. The priests and doctors have been a long time looking for the Christ. Now He is born, and the Lord has given us a sign by which to know Him. Let us go and worship Him."

And they followed the light until it came and stood over where the young Child lay. And they went in and found Mary and Joseph and the Child asleep in the sweet-smelling hay. And they worshipped Him, leaving the wee ewe lamb without spot or blemish as their offering; and returned again to their flock on the hillside, believing anew the words of the prophets.

"For unto us a Child is born. Unto us a Son is given. And the government shall be upon his shoulders; and of the increase of His Kingdom there shall be no end. And his name shall be called, 'Wonderful, Counselor, the Mighty God, the Everlasting Father, the Prince of Peace.'"✺

Tips for Lighting the Tree:
- Use one string of one hundred bulbs for each foot of the tree (4-foot tree = four strands).
- Smaller bulbs accent the tree better than larger bulbs.
- Start at the top of the tree and move downward.
- Attach the bulbs about halfway between the tips of the branches and the trunk of the tree. Use another strand to wrap around the perimeter of the tree.

CHRISTMAS TRIVIA QUIZ

A. Who tells you she's in town by tap, tap, tappin' at your windowpane?

B. What is the biggest selling Christmas single of all time?

C. What was Scrooge's first name?

D. What was the name of Rudolph's dogsled-driving friend in the claymation film *Rudolph the Red-Nosed Reindeer*?

E. In *The Night Before Christmas*, I sprang from my bed to see what?

F. Name the three reindeer whose names begin with a "D"?

G. In what city did *Miracle on 34th Street* take place?

H. Who said, "God bless us, every one"?

I. Who kept time with the Little Drummer Boy?

J. What is the last ghost called in *A Christmas Carol*?

K. In *A Charlie Brown Christmas*, who plays the dusty innkeeper in the Christmas play?

L. What did the traffic cop holler to Frosty?

M. What holiday drink contains sugar, milk, and eggs?

N. What *Saturday Evening Post* artist was known for his whimsical pictures of Santa Claus?

O. What did the Grinch use as a substitute for reindeer?

P. What were Frosty's last words?

Q. What reindeer is never mentioned in *The Night Before Christmas*?

R. What three characters sing "The Chipmunk Song"?

S. What country started the tradition of exchanging gifts?

T. What did the Little Drummer Boy give to the Christ child?

U. What popular Christmas toy is based on a 1903 political caricature?

V. After red and green, what are the two most popular Christmas colors?

W. What parade was first held on January 1, 1890?

X. What song is heard on "every street corner"?

Y. Elvis Presley recorded what sad Christmas song in the 1950s?

Z. What is the name of the most famous Christmas ballet?

Answers: A—Suzy Snowflake; B—"White Christmas"; C—Ebenezer; D—Yukon Cornelius; E—What was the matter; F—Dasher, Donner, Dancer; G—New York; H—Tiny Tim; I—The ox and the lamb; J—The Ghost of Christmas Yet to Come; K—Pigpen; L—"Stop"; M—Eggnog; N—Norman Rockwell; O—His dog; P—"I'll be back again some day"; Q—Rudolph; R—Alvin, Theodore, and Simon; S—Italy; T—He played a song on his drum; U—The Teddy Bear (President Theodore Roosevelt); V—Silver and gold; W—Tournament of Roses; X—"Silver Bells"; Y—"Blue Christmas"; Z—*The Nutcracker*

*Let's dance and sing and make good cheer,
for Christmas comes but once a year.*

G. Macfarren

SLUSH PUNCH

2 1/2 cups white sugar

6 cups water

2 (3 ounce) packages strawberry-flavored gelatin mix

1 (46 fluid ounce) can pineapple juice

2/3 cup lemon juice

1 quart orange juice

2 (2 liter) bottles lemon-lime flavored carbonated beverage

In a large saucepan, combine sugar, water, and strawberry flavored gelatin. Boil for 3 minutes. Stir in pineapple juice, lemon juice, and orange juice. Divide mixture in half, and freeze in 2 separate containers.

When ready to serve, place the frozen contents of one container in a punch bowl, and stir in 1 bottle of lemon-lime soda until slushy.

Did You Know?

Oliver Cromwell banned Christmas carols in England between 1649 and 1660. Cromwell thought that Christmas should be a very solemn day, so he banned carols and parties. The only celebration was by a sermon and a prayer service.

~

When Jesus was born in Bethlehem of Judaea in the days of Herod the king, behold, there came wise men from the east to Jerusalem, Saying, Where is he that is born King of the Jews? for we have seen his star in the east, and are come to worship him.

(Matthew 2:1–3, KJV)

~

Top Ten Favorite Christmas Gifts for Her

1. Chocolate
2. Jewelry
3. Makeup brush set
4. Pajamas
5. Handbag
6. Bathrobe
7. Favorite DVD set
8. Massage oil
9. Favorite CD
10. Bubble bath

CHRISTMAS FLOAT

1 can cola
3 scoops vanilla ice cream
4 cherries
2 red and green gumdrops
Red and green M&M's
Whipped cream topping

Put ice cream in cup. Pour cola over it. Add the whipped cream, cherries, and candy.

GOD REST YE MERRY GENTLEMEN

AUTHOR UNKNOWN

God rest ye merry gentlemen, let nothing you dismay.
Remember Christ our Savior was born on Christmas day.
To save us all from Satan's pow'r when we were gone astray;
O tidings of comfort and joy,
Comfort and joy,
O tidings of comfort and joy.

In Bethlehem, in Israel, this blessed Babe was born,
And laid within a manger upon this blessed morn;
The which His mother Mary did nothing take in scorn.
O tidings of comfort and joy,
Comfort and joy,
O tidings of comfort and joy.

From God our heavenly Father, a blessed angel came.
And unto certain shepherds brought tidings of the same,
How that in Bethlehem was born the Son of God by name;
O tidings of comfort and joy,
Comfort and joy,
O tidings of comfort and joy.

"Fear not," then said the angel, "Let nothing you affright,
This day is born a Savior, of virtue, power, and might;
So frequently to vanquish all the friends of Satan quite;"
O tidings of comfort and joy,
Comfort and joy,
O tidings of comfort and joy.

The shepherds at those tidings rejoiced much in mind,

And left their flocks a-feeding in tempest, storm, and wind,

And went to Bethlehem straight-way this blessed babe to find;

O tidings of comfort and joy,

Comfort and joy,

O tidings of comfort and joy.

But when to Bethlehem they came, whereat this infant lay,

They found him in a manger, where oxen feed on hay;

His mother Mary kneeling unto the Lord did pray:

O tidings of comfort and joy,

Comfort and joy,

O tidings of comfort and joy.

Now to the Lord sing praises all you within this place,

And with true love and brotherhood, each other now embrace;

This holy tide of Christmas all others doth deface:

O tidings of comfort and joy,

Comfort and joy,

O tidings of comfort and joy.

HISTORICAL NOTE:

The words of "God Rest Ye Merry Gentlemen," one of the oldest and most famous carols of all time, are routinely misinterpreted by those who have listened to it and sung it countless times. Through the centuries, the meaning of the words in the title have drastically changed. In fact, the title should be something like this: "God Keep You Mighty Gentlemen." So ingrained are these ancient carols that most people sing them without once questioning the odd mental picture created by this title—that of a number of happy gentlemen resting quietly under God's watchful eye.

Joseph's Letter Home

Dr. Ralph F. Wilson

*D*ear Mom,

We're still in Bethlehem—Mary and I and little Jesus.

There were lots of things I couldn't talk to you about last summer. You wouldn't have believed me then, but maybe I can tell you now. I hope you can understand.

You know, Mom, I've always loved Mary. You and dad used to tease me about her when she was still a girl. She and her brothers used to play on our street. Our families got together for supper. But the hardest day of my life came scarcely a year ago when I was twenty and she only fifteen. You remember that day, don't you?

The trouble started after we were betrothed and signed the marriage agreement at our engagement. That same spring Mary had left abruptly to visit her old cousin Elizabeth in Judea. She was gone three whole months. After she got back, people started wondering out loud if she were pregnant.

It was cloudy the day when I finally confronted her with the gossip. "Mary," I asked at last, "are you going to have a baby?"

Her clear brown eyes met mine. She nodded.

I didn't know what to say. "Who?" I finally stammered.

Mom, Mary and I had never acted improperly—even after we were betrothed.

Mary looked down. "Joseph," she said. "There's no way I can explain. You couldn't understand. But I want you to know I've never cared for anyone but you." She got up, gently took my hands in hers, kissed each of them as if it were the last time she would ever do that again, and then turned toward home. She must have been dying inside. I know I was.

The rest of the day I stumbled through my chores. It's a wonder I didn't hurt myself in the woodshop. At first I was angry and pounded out my frustrations on the doorframe I was making. My thoughts whirled so fast I could hardly keep my mind on my work. At last I decided just to end the marriage contract with a quiet divorce. I loved her too much to make a public scene.

I couldn't talk to you. Or anyone, for that matter. I went to bed early and tried to sleep. Her words came to me over and over. "I've never cared for anyone but you—I've never cared for anyone but you—" How I wished I could believe her!

I don't know when I finally fell asleep. Mom, I had a dream from God. An angel of the Lord came to me. His words pulsated through my mind so intensely I can remember them as if it were yesterday.

"Joseph, son of David," he thundered, "do not fear to take Mary home as your wife, because what is conceived in her is from the Holy Spirit."

I couldn't believe my ears, Mom. This was the answer! The angel continued, "She will give birth to a son, and you are to give him the name Jesus, because he will save his people from their sins."

The angel gripped my shoulders with his huge hands. For a long moment his gaze pierced deep within me. Just as he turned to go, I think I saw a smile on his shining face.

I sat bolt upright in bed. No sleep after that! I tossed about for a while, going over the words in my mind. Then I got up and dressed quietly so I wouldn't wake you.

I must have walked for miles beneath the moonless sky. Stars pricked the blackness like a thousand tiny pinpoints. A warm breeze blew on my face.

I sang to the Lord, Mom. Yes, me, singing, if you can imagine that. I couldn't contain my joy. I told Him that I would take Mary and care for her. I told Him I would watch over her—and the child—no matter what anyone said.

I got back just as the sun kissed the hilltops. I don't know if you still recall that morning, Mom. I can see it in my mind's eye as if it were yesterday. You were feeding the chickens, surprised to see me out. Remember?

"Sit down," I said to you. "I've got to tell you something." I took your arm and helped you find a seat on the big rock out back. "Mom," I said, "I'm going to bring Mary home as my wife. Can you help make a place for her things?"

You were silent a long time. "You do know what they're saying, don't you, son?" you said at last, your eyes glistening.

"Yes, Mom, I know."

Your voice started to rise. "If your father were still alive, he'd have some words, I'll tell you. Going about like that before you are married. Disgracing the family and all. You ... you and Mary ought to be ashamed of yourselves!"

You'd never have believed me if I'd tried to explain, so I didn't. Unless the angel had spoken to you, you'd have laughed me to scorn.

"Mom, this is the right thing to do," I said.

And then I started talking to you as if I were the head of the house. "When she comes I don't want one word to her about it," I sputtered. "She's your daughter-in-law, you'll respect her. She'll need your help if she's to bear the neighbors' wagging tongues!"

I'm sorry, Mom. You didn't deserve that. You started to get up in a huff.

"Mom," I murmured, "I need you." You took my hand and got to your feet, but the fire was gone from your eyes.

"You can count on me, Joseph," you told me with a long hug. And you meant it. I never heard another word. No bride could hope for a better mother-in-law than you those next few months.

Mom, after I left you I went up the road to Mary's house and knocked. Her mother glared at me as she opened the door. Loudly, harshly she called into the house, "It's Joseph!" almost spitting out my name as she said it.

My little Mary came out cringing, as if she expected me to give her the back of my hand, I suppose. Her eyes were red and puffy. I can just imagine what her parents had said.

We walked a few steps from the house. She looked so young and afraid. "Pack your things, Mary," I told her gently. "I'm taking you home to be my wife."

"Joseph!" She hugged me as tight as she could. Mom, I didn't realize she was so strong.

I told her what I'd been planning. "We'll go to Rabbi Ben-Ezer's house this week and have him perform the ceremony."

I know it was awfully sudden, Mom, but I figured the sooner we got married the better it would be for her, and me, and the baby.

"Mary, even if our friends don't come, at least you and I can pledge our love before God." I paused. "I think my mom will be there. And maybe your friend Rebecca would come if her dad will let her. How about your parents?"

I could feel Mary's tiny frame shuddering as she sobbed quietly.

"Mary," I said. I could feel myself speaking more boldly. "No matter what anyone says about you, I'm proud you're going to be my wife. I'm going to take good care of you. I've promised God that."

She looked up.

I lowered my voice. "I had a dream last night, Mary. I saw an angel. I know."

The anguish that had gripped her face vanished. She was radiant as we turned away from the house and began to walk up the hill together.

Just then her mother ran out into the yard. "Wait," she called. She must have been listening from behind the door. Tears were streaming down her cheeks.

"I'll get your father," she called, almost giddy with emotion. "We," she cried as she gathered up her skirts. "We," she shouted as she began to run to find her husband. "We ... are going to have a wedding!"

That's how it was, Mom. Thanks for being there for us. I'll write again soon.

Love, Joseph[10] ✶

The joy of brightening each others' lives,
bearing each others' burdens, easing each others' loads and
supplanting empty hearts and lives with
generous gifts becomes for us the
magic of Christmas.

W. C. JONES

December 23

*The hinge of history
is on the door of a Bethlehem stable.*

Ralph Sockman

A VISIT FROM THE CHRIST CHILD

BY PÈRE ROBÉRT

FOR MARIA, IDA, ISABEL, MAXINE, CROZET & AUDREY

Twas the morning of Christmas, when all through the house
All the family was frantic, including my spouse;
For each one of them had one thing only in mind,
To examine the presents St. Nick left behind.

The boxes and wrapping and ribbons and toys
Were strewn on the floor, and the volume of noise
Increased as our children began a big fight
Over who got the video games, who got the bike.

I looked at my watch and I said, slightly nervous,
"Let's get ready for church, so we won't miss the service."
The children protested, "We don't want to pray:
We've just got our presents, and we want to play!"

It dawned on me then that we had gone astray,
In confusing the purpose of this special day;
Our presents were many and very high-priced
But something was missing—that something was Christ!
I said, "Put the gifts down and let's gather together,
And I'll tell you a tale of the greatest gift ever.

"A savior was promised when Adam first sinned,
And the hopes of the world upon Jesus were pinned.
Abraham begat Isaac, who Jacob begat,

And through David the line went to Joseph, whereat
This carpenter married a maiden with child,
Who yet was a virgin, in no way defiled.

"Saying 'Hail, full of Grace,' an archangel appeared
To Mary the Blessed, among women revered:
The Lord willed she would bear—through the Spirit—a son.
Said Mary to Gabriel, 'God's will be done.'

"Now Caesar commanded a tax would be paid,
And all would go home while the census was made;
Thus Joseph and Mary did leave Galilee
For the city of David to pay this new fee.

"Mary's time had arrived, but the inn had no room,
So she laid in a manger the fruit of her womb;
And both Joseph and Mary admired as He napped
The Light of the World in his swaddling clothes wrapped.

"Three wise men from the East had come looking for news
Of the birth of the Savior, the King of the Jews;
They carried great gifts as they followed a star—
Gold, frankincense, myrrh, which they'd brought from afar.

"As the shepherds watched over their flocks on that night,
The glory of God shone upon them quite bright,
And an angel explained the intent of the birth,
Saying, 'Glory to God and His peace to the earth.'

"For this was the Messiah whom prophets foretold,
A good shepherd to bring his sheep back to the fold;
He was God become man, He would die on the cross,
He would rise from the dead to restore Adam's loss.

"Santa Claus, Christmas presents, a brightly lit pine,
Candy canes and spiked eggnog are all very fine;
Let's have fun celebrating, but leave not a doubt
That Christ is what Christmas is really about!"

The children right then put an end to the noise,
They dressed quickly for church, put away all their toys;
For they knew Jesus loved them and said they were glad
That He'd died for their sins, and to save their dear Dad.[11]

CHRISTMAS EVE

SAMUEL TAYLOR COLERIDGE

On the evening before Christmas Day, one of the parlors is lighted up by the children, into which the parents must not go; a great yew bough is fastened on the table at a distance from the wall, a multitude of little tapers are fixed to the bough, but not so as to burn it till they are nearly consumed, and colored paper, etc., hangs and flutters from the twigs.

Under this bough the children lay out in great order the presents they mean to give their parents, still concealing in their pockets what they intend to give each other. Then the parents are introduced, and each presents his little gift; they then bring out the remainder one by one, from their pockets and present them with kisses and embraces. I was very much affected. The shadow of the bough and its appendages on the wall and arching over the ceiling made a pretty picture. ✳

CHRISTMAS DINNER IN FRANCE

Gros Souper—family meal served on Christmas Eve before leaving for Midnight Mass)

Cabbage or garlic soup

Celery with anchoade

Snail (on skewers served with aioli)

Dried cod and spinach gratin

Wild artichoke vinaigrette

Honey cake with dried fruit

Repas Gras—family meal served on Christmas Day after Midnight Mass)

Assorted game

Roasted meats

Bûche de Noël

Le Treize Desserts (13 symbolic desserts)

Wine

The History

- Almost every region in France has its own special way to celebrate the Christian holidays.
- The week before Christmas the santons—the figures of the Nativity— are unpacked and placed on the mantel or table. A little stable with the holy family is added to the table, which is already decorated with plants.
- Small plays are staged in the theaters in many small towns. These are called presepi, and each character represented by the Santons plays a part.

- On Christmas Eve, before Midnight Mass, the family gathers for the gros souper. This meal celebrates all the things the family is thankful for. Seven meatless meals are served, which represent the seven sorrows of the Virgin Mary. The table is set with three white tablecloths and three candles, representing the Trinity.
- On December 4—St. Barbe's day—children wrap wheat or lentil seeds in a damp cloth for germination. The tiny seedlings are transplanted and placed in a sunny window to grow. The plants represent prosperity for the family in the coming year and are used to decorate the crèche as well as the table for the Christmas Eve supper.
- Before gros souper, the oldest and youngest members of the family walk around the table three times carrying a fruitwood log. It is blessed with some of the wine and placed in the fireplace.
- After the gros souper, the treize desserts are served. There are thirteen, representing all those present at the Last Supper. Before leaving for Mass, the desserts are placed on a clean tablecloth at another table for neighbors and the needy to help themselves to while the family is at church.
- After Mass, the family sits down again for repas gras. This includes assorted game, roasts, and wine.

Did You Know?

- Leftover wine is poured on the fire. The yule log is removed, wrapped, and put away before Midnight Mass on Christmas Eve.
- The thirteen desserts are typically composed of: oranges from Nice, tangerines, winter melon, pears, apples, pomegranates, grapes, figs, hazelnuts, almonds, walnuts, dates, fruit, tortes, black and white nougats, pâté de coing (quince paste), candied fruits, and sweet cake enriched with orange blossom water and olive oil.

For Our French Friends: After two days of feasting, you must be glad to sit down to a simple bowl of garlic soup for Christmas dinner!

THE TEN COMMANDMENTS OF CHRISTMAS

   I. You shall not leave Christ out of Christmas.

  II. You shall prepare your soul for Christmas.

 III. You shall not let Santa Claus replace Christ.

 IV. You shall not burden the salesgirl, the mailman, and the merchant with complaints and demands.

  V. You shall give yourself with your gift.

 VI. You shall not value gifts received by their cost.

VII. You shall not neglect the needy.

VIII. You shall not neglect the church services that highlight the true meaning of the season.

 IX. You shall be as a little child.

  X. You shall give your heart to Christ.

THE TWELVE DAYS OF CHRISTMAS

AUTHOR UNKNOWN

On the first day of Christmas my true love sent to me:
A Partridge in a Pear Tree.

On the second day of Christmas my true love sent to me:
2 Turtle Doves
and a Partridge in a Pear Tree.

On the third day of Christmas my true love sent to me:
3 French Hens,
2 Turtle Doves, and a Partridge in a Pear Tree.

On the fourth day of Christmas my true love sent to me:
4 Calling Birds,
3 French Hens,
2 Turtle Doves, and a Partridge in a Pear Tree.

On the fifth day of Christmas my true love sent to me:
5 Golden Rings,
4 Calling Birds, 3 French Hens,
2 Turtle Doves, and a Partridge in a Pear Tree,

On the sixth day of Christmas my true love sent to me:
6 Geese a Laying,
5 Golden Rings, 4 Calling Birds, 3 French Hens,
2 Turtle Doves, and a Partridge in a Pear Tree.

On the seventh day of Christmas my true love sent to me:
7 Swans a Swimming,
6 Geese a Laying,
5 Golden Rings, 4 Calling Birds, 3 French Hens,

2 Turtle Doves, and a Partridge in a Pear Tree.

On the eighth day of Christmas my true love sent to me:
8 Maids a Milking,
7 Swans a Swimming, 6 Geese a Laying,
5 Golden Rings, 4 Calling Birds, 3 French Hens,
2 Turtle Doves, and a Partridge in a Pear Tree.

On the ninth day of Christmas my true love sent to me:
9 Ladies Dancing,
8 Maids a Milking, 7 Swans a Swimming, 6 Geese a Laying,
5 Golden Rings, 4 Calling Birds, 3 French Hens,
2 Turtle Doves, and a Partridge in a Pear Tree.

On the tenth day of Christmas my true love sent to me:
10 Lords a Leaping,
9 Ladies Dancing, 8 Maids a Milking, 7 Swans a Swimming,
6 Geese a Laying, 5 Golden Rings, 4 Calling Birds, 3 French Hens,
2 Turtle Doves, and a Partridge in a Pear Tree

On the eleventh day of Christmas my true love sent to me:
11 Pipers Piping,
10 Lords a Leaping, 9 Ladies Dancing,
8 Maids a Milking, 7 Swans a Swimming, 6 Geese a Laying,
5 Golden Rings, 4 Calling Birds, 3 French Hens,
2 Turtle Doves, and a Partridge in a Pear Tree.

On the twelfth day of Christmas my true love sent to me:
12 Drummers Drumming,
11 Pipers Piping, 10 Lords a Leaping, 9 Ladies Dancing,
8 Maids a Milking, 7 Swans a Swimming, 6 Geese a Laying,
5 Golden Rings, 4 Calling Birds, 3 French Hens,
2 Turtle Doves, and a Partridge in a Pear Tree.

HISTORICAL NOTE:

Legend has it that the song "The Twelve Days of Christmas" was written to help children remember the tenets of their faith. What do you think?

The true love was God Himself.

The "me" was any baptized person.

The partridge in a pear tree was Christ and may have referred to Matthew 23:37 and Luke 13:34.

The two turtle doves were the Old and New Testaments.

The three French hens stood for faith, hope, and love. (See 1 Corinthians 13.)

The four calling birds were the four gospels—Matthew, Mark, Luke, and John.

The five golden rings recalled the Torah or law: Genesis, Exodus, Leviticus, Numbers, Deuteronomy. The Pentateuch.

The six geese a laying were the six days of creation.

The seven swans a swimming were the seven Sacraments.

The eight maids a milking were the eight Beatitudes. (See Matthew 5:3-12.)

The nine ladies dancing represented the fruit of the Holy Spirit. (See Galatians 5:22-23.)

The ten Lords a leaping were the Ten Commandments.

The eleven pipers piping were the eleven faithful apostles.

The twelve drummers drumming symbolized the twelve points of belief in the Apostle's Creed.

Are you willing to believe that love is the strongest thing in the world—stronger than hate, stronger than evil, stronger than death—and that the blessed life which began in Bethlehem nineteen hundred years ago is the image and brightness of the Eternal Love? Then you can keep Christmas.

HENRY VAN DYKE

December 24

The universal joy of Christmas is certainly wonderful.
We ring the bells when princes are born, or toll a mournful dirge
when great men pass away. Nations have their red-letter days,
their carnivals and festivals, but once in the year, and only once,
the whole world stands still to celebrate the advent of a life.
Only Jesus of Nazareth claims this worldwide,
undying remembrance. You cannot cut Christmas
out of the calendar, nor out of
the heart of the world.

AUTHOR UNKNOWN

'TWAS THE NIGHT BEFORE CHRISTMAS

CLEMENT CLARKE MOORE

'Twas the night before Christmas, when all through the house
Not a creature was stirring, not even a mouse.
The stockings were hung by the chimney with care,
In hopes that St. Nicholas soon would be there.

The children were nestled all snug in their beds,
While visions of sugar-plums danced in their heads.
And mamma in her 'kerchief, and I in my cap,
Had just settled our brains for a long winter's nap.

When out on the lawn there arose such a clatter,
I sprang from the bed to see what was the matter.
Away to the window I flew like a flash,
Tore open the shutters and threw up the sash.

The moon on the breast of the new-fallen snow
Gave the lustre of mid-day to objects below.
When, what to my wondering eyes should appear,
But a miniature sleigh, and eight tiny reindeer.

With a little old driver, so lively and quick,
I knew in a moment it must be St. Nick.
More rapid than eagles his coursers they came,
And he whistled, and shouted, and called them by name!

"Now Dasher! Now, Dancer! Now, Prancer and Vixen!
On, Comet! On, Cupid! On, Donner and Blitzen!
To the top of the porch! to the top of the wall!

Now dash away! Dash away! Dash away all!"

As dry leaves that before the wild hurricane fly,
When they meet with an obstacle, mount to the sky.
So up to the house-top the coursers they flew,
With the sleigh full of toys, and St. Nicholas too.

And then, in a twinkling, I heard on the roof
The prancing and pawing of each little hoof.
As I drew in my head, and was turning around,
Down the chimney St. Nicholas came with a bound.

He was dressed all in fur, from his head to his foot,
And his clothes were all tarnished with ashes and soot.
A bundle of toys he had flung on his back,
And he looked like a peddler, just opening his pack.

His eyes—how they twinkled! His dimples how merry!
His cheeks were like roses, his nose like a cherry!
His droll little mouth was drawn up like a bow,
And the beard of his chin was as white as the snow.

The stump of a pipe he held tight in his teeth,
And the smoke it encircled his head like a wreath.
He had a broad face and a little round belly,
That shook when he laughed, like a bowlful of jelly!

He was chubby and plump, a right jolly old elf,
And I laughed when I saw him, in spite of myself!
A wink of his eye and a twist of his head,
Soon gave me to know I had nothing to dread.

He spoke not a word, but went straight to his work,
And filled all the stockings, then turned with a jerk.

And laying his finger aside of his nose,
And giving a nod, up the chimney he rose!

He sprang to his sleigh, to his team gave a whistle,
And away they all flew like the down of a thistle.
But I heard him exclaim, 'ere he drove out of sight,
"Happy Christmas to all, and to all a good-night!"

Top Ten Favorite Christmas Gifts for Him

1. Blu-ray player
2. Camera
3. Guitar
4. Favorite Xbox 360 or PS3 game
5. Jewelry
6. Favorite DVD
7. Cologne
8. Leather wallet
9. Favorite CD
10. Pajamas

Did You Know?

Gift giving was first practiced by the Romans, who customarily exchanged small gifts during the winter months. The Christmas gift giving we know probably began when early Christians, inspired by the belief that the shepherds and Magi took gifts to the Christ child, began to observe the custom.

Christmas Breakfast Casserole

12-ounce package frozen hash browns

1/4 cup melted butter

1 cup diced ham

4 ounces cheddar cheese, shredded

4 ounces Swiss cheese, shredded

4-ounce can diced green chilies

2 eggs

1/2 cup milk

1/4 tsp. salt

Salsa

Spread hash browns in a 10-inch pie pan greased with butter. Brush with melted butter and bake at 425°F for 25 minutes. Layer ham, cheeses, and chilies on top of hash browns. Combine eggs, milk, and salt. Pour over ham, cheese, and chilies. Bake at 350°F for 30–35 minutes. Makes 6–8 servings.

SING WE ALL MERRILY

OLD COLONIAL CHRISTMAS SONG

Sing we all merrily, Christmas is here,
The day that we love best of days of the year.
Bring forth the holly, the box, and the bay,
Deck out our cottage for glad Christmas Day.
Sing we all merrily, draw around the fire,
Sister and brother, grandsire, and sire.

*The Christmas message is
that there is hope for a ruined humanity—
hope of pardon, hope of peace with God,
hope of glory—because at the Father's will
Jesus Christ became poor, and was born in a stable so that
thirty years later He might hang on a cross.*

J. I. PACKER

THE STORY OF THE CHRIST CHILD

*C*hristmas is a celebration of the incarnation, not just the nativity. The real celebration should not be just about His birth but also the fact that God chose to become a man so that He might bring salvation to mankind. The Baby born in Bethlehem grew up and sacrificed His life as a payment for our sin. What a Savior!

These are words to remember as the story of that remarkable event is told. As you read, imagine how His story—His coming—has touched all the corners of your life!

LUKE 1; 2:1–40, MSG

So many others have tried their hand at putting together a story of the wonderful harvest of Scripture and history that took place among us, using reports handed down by the original eyewitnesses who served this Word with their very lives. Since I have investigated all the reports in close detail, starting from the story's beginning, I decided to write it all out for you, most honorable Theophilus, so you can know beyond the shadow of a doubt the reliability of what you were taught.

A CHILDLESS COUPLE CONCEIVES

During the rule of Herod, King of Judea, there was a priest assigned service in the regiment of Abijah. His name was Zachariah. His wife was descended from the daughters of Aaron. Her name was Elizabeth. Together they lived honorably before God, careful in keeping to the ways of the commandments and enjoying a clear conscience before God. But they were childless because Elizabeth could never conceive, and now they were quite old.

It so happened that as Zachariah was carrying out his priestly duties before God, working the shift assigned to his regiment, it came his one turn in life to enter the sanctuary of God and burn incense. The congregation was gathered and praying outside the Temple at the hour of the incense offering. Unannounced, an angel of God appeared just to the right of the altar of incense. Zachariah was paralyzed in fear.

But the angel reassured him, "Don't fear, Zachariah. Your prayer has been heard. Elizabeth, your wife, will bear a son by you. You are to name him John. You're going to leap like a gazelle for joy, and not only you—many will delight in his birth. He'll achieve great stature with God.

"He'll drink neither wine nor beer. He'll be filled with the Holy Spirit from the moment he leaves his mother's womb. He will turn many sons and daughters of Israel back to their God. He will herald God's arrival in the style and strength of Elijah, soften the hearts of parents to children, and kindle devout understanding among hardened skeptics—he'll get the people ready for God."

Zachariah said to the angel, "Do you expect me to believe this? I'm an old man and my wife is an old woman."

But the angel said, "I am Gabriel, the sentinel of God, sent especially to bring you this glad news. But because you won't believe me, you'll be unable to say a word until the day of your son's birth. Every word I've spoken to you will come true on time—*God's* time."

Meanwhile, the congregation waiting for Zachariah was getting restless, wondering what was keeping him so long in the sanctuary. When he came out and couldn't speak, they knew he had seen a vision. He continued speechless and had to use sign language with the people.

When the course of his priestly assignment was completed, he went back home. It wasn't long before his wife, Elizabeth, conceived. She went off by herself for five months, relishing her pregnancy. "So, this is how God acts to remedy my unfortunate condition!" she said.

A VIRGIN CONCEIVES

In the sixth month of Elizabeth's pregnancy, God sent the angel Gabriel to the Galilean village of Nazareth to a virgin engaged to be married to a man descended from David. His name was Joseph, and the virgin's name, Mary. Upon entering, Gabriel greeted her:

> Good morning!
> You're beautiful with God's beauty,
> Beautiful inside and out!
> God be with you.

She was thoroughly shaken, wondering what was behind a greeting like that. But the angel assured her, "Mary, you have nothing to fear. God has a surprise for you: You will become pregnant and give birth to a son and call his name Jesus.

> He will be great,
>   be called 'Son of the Highest.'
> The Lord God will give him
>   the throne of his father David;
> He will rule Jacob's house forever—
>   no end, ever, to his kingdom."

Mary said to the angel, "But how? I've never slept with a man."
The angel answered,

> The Holy Spirit will come upon you,
>   the power of the Highest hover over you;
> Therefore, the child you bring to birth
>   will be called Holy, Son of God.

And did you know that your cousin Elizabeth conceived a son, old as she is? Everyone called her barren, and here she is six months' pregnant! Nothing, you see, is impossible with God."

And Mary said,

> Yes, I see it all now:
>> I'm the Lord's maid, ready to serve.
> Let it be with me
>> just as you say.

Then the angel left her.

BLESSED AMONG WOMEN

Mary didn't waste a minute. She got up and traveled to a town in Judah in the hill country, straight to Zachariah's house, and greeted Elizabeth. When Elizabeth heard Mary's greeting, the baby in her womb leaped. She was filled with the Holy Spirit, and sang out exuberantly,

> You're so blessed among women,
>> and the babe in your womb, also blessed!
> And why am I so blessed that
>> the mother of my Lord visits me?
> The moment the sound of your
>> greeting entered my ears,
> The babe in my womb
>> skipped like a lamb for sheer joy.
> Blessed woman, who believed what God said,
>> believed every word would come true!

And Mary said,

> I'm bursting with God-news;
>> I'm dancing the song of my Savior God.

God took one good look at me, and look what happened—
>   I'm the most fortunate woman on earth!
What God has done for me will never be forgotten,
>   the God whose very name is holy, set apart from all others.
His mercy flows in wave after wave
>   on those who are in awe before him.
He bared his arm and showed his strength,
>   scattered the bluffing braggarts.
He knocked tyrants off their high horses,
pulled victims out of the mud.
The starving poor sat down to a banquet;
>   the callous rich were left out in the cold.
He embraced his chosen child, Israel;
>   he remembered and piled on the mercies, piled them high.
It's exactly what he promised,
>   beginning with Abraham and right up to now.

Mary stayed with Elizabeth for three months and then went back to her own home.

THE BIRTH OF JOHN

When Elizabeth was full-term in her pregnancy, she bore a son. Her neighbors and relatives, seeing that God had overwhelmed her with mercy, celebrated with her.

On the eighth day, they came to circumcise the child and were calling him Zachariah after his father. But his mother intervened: "No. He is to be called John."

"But," they said, "no one in your family is named that." They used sign language to ask Zachariah what he wanted him named.

Asking for a tablet, Zachariah wrote, "His name is to be John." That took everyone by surprise. Surprise followed surprise—Zachariah's mouth was now open, his tongue loose, and he was talking, praising God!

A deep, reverential fear settled over the neighborhood, and in all that Judean hill country people talked about nothing else. Everyone who heard about it took it to heart, wondering, "What will become of this child? Clearly, God has his hand in this."

Then Zachariah was filled with the Holy Spirit and prophesied,

> Blessed be the Lord, the God of Israel;
> > he came and set his people free.
> He set the power of salvation in the center of our lives,
> > and in the very house of David his servant,
> Just as he promised long ago
> > through the preaching of his holy prophets:
> Deliverance from our enemies
> > and every hateful hand;
> Mercy to our fathers,
> > as he remembers to do what he said he'd do,
> What he swore to our father Abraham—
> > a clean rescue from the enemy camp,
> So we can worship him without a care in the world,
> > made holy before him as long as we live.
>
> And you, my child, "Prophet of the Highest,"
> > will go ahead of the Master to prepare his ways,
> Present the offer of salvation to his people,
> > the forgiveness of their sins.
> Through the heartfelt mercies of our God,
> > God's Sunrise will break in upon us,
> Shining on those in the darkness,
> > those sitting in the shadow of death,

Then showing us the way, one foot at a time,
down the path of peace.

The child grew up, healthy and spirited. He lived out in the desert until the day he made his prophetic debut in Israel.

THE BIRTH OF JESUS

About that time Caesar Augustus ordered a census to be taken throughout the Empire. This was the first census when Quirinus was governor of Syria. Everyone had to travel to his own ancestral hometown to be accounted for. So Joseph went from the Galilean town of Nazareth up to Bethlehem in Judah, David's town, for the census. As a descendant of David, he had to go there. He went with Mary, his fiancée, who was pregnant.

While they were there, the time came for her to give birth. She gave birth to a son, her firstborn. She wrapped him in a blanket and laid him in a manger, because there was no room in the hostel.

AN EVENT FOR EVERYONE

There were sheepherders camping in the neighborhood. They had set night watches over their sheep. Suddenly, God's angel stood among them and God's glory blazed around them. They were terrified. The angel said, "Don't be afraid. I'm here to announce a great and joyful event that is meant for everybody, worldwide: A Savior has just been born in David's town, a Savior who is Messiah and Master. This is what you're to look for: a baby wrapped in a blanket and lying in a manger."

At once the angel was joined by a huge angelic choir singing God's praises:

Glory to God in the heavenly heights,
Peace to all men and women on earth who please him.

As the angel choir withdrew into heaven, the sheepherders talked it over. "Let's get over to Bethlehem as fast as we can and see for ourselves what God has revealed to us." They left, running, and found Mary and Joseph, and the baby lying in the manger. Seeing was believing. They told everyone they met what the angels had said about this child. All who heard the sheepherders were impressed.

Mary kept all these things to herself, holding them dear, deep within herself. The sheepherders returned and let loose, glorifying and praising God for everything they had heard and seen. It turned out exactly the way they'd been told!

BLESSINGS

When the eighth day arrived, the day of circumcision, the child was named Jesus, the name given by the angel before he was conceived.

Then when the days stipulated by Moses for purification were complete, they took him up to Jerusalem to offer him to God as commanded in God's Law: "Every male who opens the womb shall be a holy offering to God," and also to sacrifice the "pair of doves or two young pigeons" prescribed in God's Law.

In Jerusalem at the time, there was a man, Simeon by name, a good man, a man who lived in the prayerful expectancy of help for Israel. And the Holy Spirit was on him. The Holy Spirit had shown him that he would see the Messiah of God before he died. Led by the Spirit, he entered the Temple. As the parents of the child Jesus brought him in to carry out the rituals of the Law, Simeon took him into his arms and blessed God:

> God, you can now release your servant;
>> release me in peace as you promised.
> With my own eyes I've seen your salvation;
>> it's now out in the open for everyone to see:

> A God-revealing light to the non-Jewish nations,
>> and of glory for your people Israel.

Jesus' father and mother were speechless with surprise at these words. Simeon went on to bless them, and said to Mary his mother,

> This child marks both the failure and
>> the recovery of many in Israel,
> A figure misunderstood and contradicted—
>> the pain of a sword-thrust through you—
> But the rejection will force honesty,
>> as God reveals who they really are.

Anna the prophetess was also there, a daughter of Phanuel from the tribe of Asher. She was by now a very old woman. She had been married seven years and a widow for eighty-four. She never left the Temple area, worshiping night and day with her fastings and prayers. At the very time Simeon was praying, she showed up, broke into an anthem of praise to God, and talked about the child to all who were waiting expectantly for the freeing of Jerusalem.

When they finished everything required by God in the Law, they returned to Galilee and their own town, Nazareth. There the child grew strong in body and wise in spirit. And the grace of God was on him. ✳

POST-CHRISTMAS PRAYER

AUTHOR UNKNOWN

Long after the angels disappear into the heavens, the shepherds return to their flocks, the magi journey home, and the great star sets, Jesus remains.

The Child in whom we rediscover God's great love for humanity becomes the adult Redeemer who challenges us to imitate his selflessness and compassion in order that we might transform our world in love.

May we allow the miracle of Christmas to continue long after the holiday trappings have been packed away.

May we welcome the adult Messiah and his challenging Gospel to recreate our lives—making the peace, justice, and hope of this holy season a reality in every season of the new year.

INDEX

Christmas Quotations by:

Christmas Recipes

Christmas Scriptures

Christmas Songs, Carols, and Hymns

Christmas Stories

Christmas Traditions

Christmas Trivia and Humor

NOTES

1. *Unlikely Places* by Cheri Fuller, a Gold Medallion award–winning author and speaker. Learn more about Cheri at www.cherifuller.com. This story is used by permission of the author.

2. *A Refugee Camp Christmas* by Renie Burghardt, Doniphan, Missouri. Used by permission of the author.

3. *Bill for the Twelve Days of Christmas Gifts*. Joyful Noiseletter. Copyright © Fellowship of Merry Christians, P. O. Box 895, Portage, MI 49081-0895, www.joyfulnoiseletter.com

4. "God Jul!" by Marilyn Jazkulke. Mission Viejo, California. Used by permission of the author.

5. *The Tiniest Miracle* by Bonnie Compton Hanson, Santa Ana, California. Used by permission of the author.

6. *Paper Sack Christmas* by Elece Hollis. Used by permission of the author.

7. *Balmy Clergy Supply Gifts for Clergy* composed by Rev. David R. Francoeur, consulting editor of Joyful Noiseletter, copyright © Fellowship of Merry Christians, P.O Box 895, Portage, MI 49081-0895, www.joyfulnoiseletter.com

8. *Smithsonian Magazine* (December 2005, pp25ff)

9. *Out of the Mouths of Babes*. Joyful Noiseletter. Copyright © Fellowship of Merry Christians, P.O. Box 895, Portage, MI 49081-0895, www.joyfulnoiseletter.com

10. *Joseph's Letter Home* by Dr. Ralph Wilson. Used by permission of the author.

11. ©1986 F.R. Duplantier http://www.politickles.com/thankevann/christchild/ Used by permission as noted on the Web site.